Crescent City Moons Dishes and Spoons

The Junior League of New Orleans, Inc., is an organization of women committed to promoting voluntarism, developing the potential of women, and improving communities through the effective action and leadership of trained volunteers. Its purpose is exclusively educational and charitable.

Crescent City Moons, Dishes and Spoons for the growing chef

Published by The Junior League of New Orleans, Inc.
Copyright © 2010

The Junior League of New Orleans, Inc.
4319 Carondelet
New Orleans, Louisiana 70115
504.891.5845

Photography: © Natalie Root Photography
Illustrations: Wendy Bridevaux
Stylist: Virginia "Ginja" Duncan Moseley

Library of Congress Control Number: 2009923838
ISBN: 978-0-9604774-5-6

Edited, Designed, and Produced by

(||) Favorite Recipes® Press

an imprint of

FRP.INC

A wholly owned subsidiary of Southwestern/Great American, Inc.
P.O. Box 305142
Nashville, Tennessee 37230
800.358.0560

Art Director and Book Design: Steve Newman
Project Editor: Debbie Van Mol

Manufactured in the United States of America
First Printing: 2010
15,000 copies

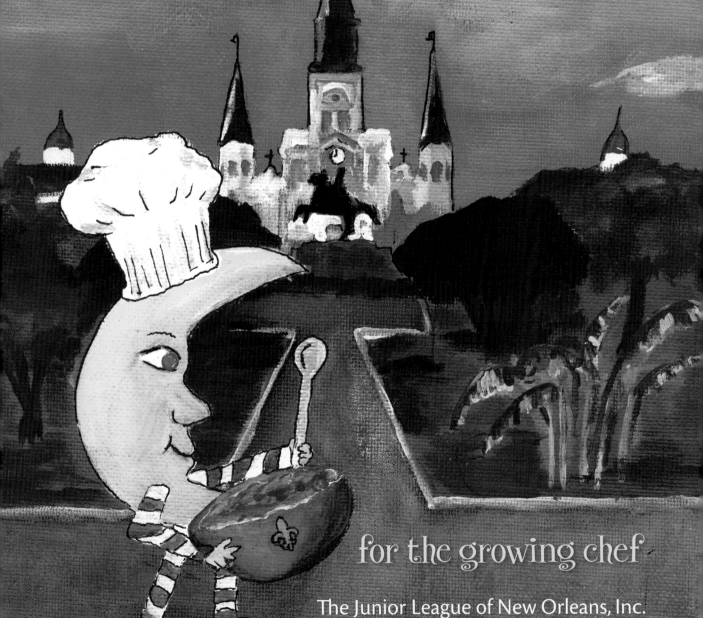

Crescent City Moons Dishes and Spoons

for the growing chef

The Junior League of New Orleans, Inc.

About the...

...Artist Wendy Bridevaux is an artist and teacher. She teaches elementary school during the school year and art lessons over the summer. On weekends Wendy sells her paintings on Jackson Square in the French Quarter. She was born and raised in Metairie, Louisiana, and attended Louisiana State University, where she received a Master's degree in elementary education with a concentration in painting and drawing.

...Photographer Natalie Root is a freelance editorial and commercial food photographer in New Orleans. Her work appears in several regional magazines, contributing to the recipe sections, as well as covering restaurants and food events. She has her own series of art for the kitchen, "New Orleans Fare," which celebrates classic New Orleans iconic food. She is an alumna of Loyola University New Orleans.

...Stylist Virginia (Ginja) Duncan Moseley assisted as the stylist for the photo shoots. As an interior designer, florist, and party and wedding planner she has sharpened her eye over the years as a contributing editor to *Southern Accents*. She has also contributed to *St. Charles Avenue* and *Louisiana Homes and Lifestyles* as a freelance editor. Her work has appeared in both publications. Her hobbies include cooking, photography, and jewelry design.

The Junior League of
New Orleans, Inc.

Since its founding in 1924 by ten civic-minded women, The Junior League of
New Orleans, Inc., has served the New Orleans community through the effective action
and leadership of trained volunteers. The Junior League of New Orleans, Inc.,
has been involved with well over one hundred different community projects addressing
children's education, health initiatives, welfare and recreation for all ages, and
many other collaborative efforts in support of building a better New Orleans community.
Members of The Junior League of New Orleans, Inc., volunteer in excess of
50,000 hours of their time annually.

The following programs began as The Junior League of New Orleans, Inc., projects:
the Preservation Resource Center of New Orleans, the Parenting Center at
Children's Hospital, the Louisiana Nature and Science Center, Teen Court for Orleans
and Jefferson Parishes, the Holman Vocational Center, and many other
noteworthy programs in our city.

As of publication, our chapter holds a membership of more than 2,100 women volunteers,
making The Junior League of New Orleans, Inc., the eleventh largest League in the world.
The Junior League of New Orleans, Inc., is an organization of women committed to
promoting voluntarism, developing the potential of women, and improving communities
through the effective action and leadership of trained volunteers.
Its purpose is exclusively educational and charitable.

Your purchase of *Crescent City Moons, Dishes and Spoons* helps guarantee the continued
success of The Junior League of New Orleans, Inc., in training member volunteers and
leaders, developing the potential of women, and improving our communities.

Original Cookbook Committee

2008–2009

Chair	Cris Bregman
Recipe Chairs	Amy Gutierrez
	Susan Taylor
Photography/Art Chair	Cheryl Webster
Marketing Chairs	Jeanea Bandi
	Caroline Wendt
Non-Recipe Text	Cris Bregman
	Elesha Kelleher
Nutritional Analysis	Phoebe Cook
Committee Members	Jennifer DiGiovanni
	Helen Fish
	Allison McCammon
	Annie Phillips
	Jodie Trask
	Courtney Walker
Sustainer Advisor	Lyn Hallaron
Council Directors	Carolyn Hennesy
	Hallie White

The Junior League of New Orleans, Inc.

Presidents

Gwathmey Finlay Gomila	Leah Nunn Engelhardt	Erin Bell Luetkemeier
2007–2008	2008–2009	2009–2010

Photography Set-Up/Design

Elizabeth Berger

Reed Bowman

Cris Bregman

Callie Daters

Leah Engelhardt

Nancy Falgoust

Skye Fantaci

Helen Fish

Traci Hamann

Heather Johnson

Holt Kolb

Ann Koppel

Megan Layman

Tara Luparello

Melissa Mantilla

Vanessa Martin

Allison McCammon

Ryan Miller

Anne Mitchell-Wypyski

Ginja Moseley

Michelle Nickerson

Sherri Zeller O'Bell

Rachel O'Dwyer

Annie Phillips

Robyn Schwarz

Susan Taylor

Jodie Trask

Cheryl Webster

Caroline Wendt

Julia Wessman

Hallie White

Photographed Homes

Edward and Lisa Ludwig

Hans and Erin Luetkemeier

Nathaniel and Annie Phillips

Contents

18
Crescent City
Coos

36
Crescent City
Cuties

70
Crescent City
Cool Kids

Preface 10

Foreword 12

Introduction 15

Sponsors 224

Chef Contributors 225

Contributors List 226

Junior Taste Testers 228

Recipe Basics 229

Nutritional Profiles 230

Index 234

Order Information 239

112
Crescent City
Celebrations

146
Crescent City
Cultures

176
Crescent City
Chefs

202
Crescent City Conditional Cooking

Preface

As an adult with children of my own, I recognize that growing up, I was privileged—privileged to be raised on a family farm in a small Alabama town. On the "Nunn Homeplace," dinner (lunch in the South) and supper (dinner in the South) started with a simple request to head out to the garden to choose the next meal. In the summer, I had my pick of varieties of fresh vegetables and fruits, and sometimes even flowers for the table. During the winter, my selections came from the winter garden out back and what was canned or frozen at summer's end. Despite the frequent mess, my father's command of the kitchen ensured that nothing went to waste.

Not realizing it at the time (and perhaps not until well into my adult life) I was a *growing chef*. During the summer months, I shared in the preparation of meals by snapping beans and shelling butter beans and purple hull peas. In the winter we collected greens of all kinds and washed potatoes. We had family breakfast each morning and supper each night. Sunday dinner was a given. Yes, I was privileged to have these opportunities to be a *growing chef*—a chef with the best of the best ingredients to choose from and work with. Right there in my own backyard.

Today, through over eighty-five years of community involvement, especially dedicated to working with children of the New Orleans community, The Junior League of New Orleans, Inc., knows that many children and families will not grow up with a garden out back and adult "chefs" at home to help mentor healthful choices, cooking, and eating. From its community initiatives in improving children's education and from addressing urgent issues surrounding childhood obesity and poor nutrition, the League knows that families will benefit from this collective source of healthful recipes and eating and living tips. This book is an enjoyable resource that encourages families to gather in the kitchen and at the table. Although perhaps unseen at the time, the rewards will last long after meals are shared and tables cleared.

Few readers understand the need for this cookbook better than Children's Cookbook Chair Cris Bregman, who transferred to The Junior League of New Orleans, Inc., soon after Hurricane Katrina. She notes, "When I first learned the League was considering publication of a cookbook dedicated to children, families together, and healthy eating, I knew I was here for a reason. My passion is children's education, and cooking with my own children is a hobby." Through Cris's dedication, detailed research, and perseverance to provide families with a quality resource unmatched by any other, this consideration is now a reality.

Susan Johnson, a Junior League of New Orleans, Inc., sustaining member and past Cookbook Committee Chair who launched the League's award-winning *Jambalaya* cookbook, knows well the challenges inherent in producing a cookbook, but calls attention to the importance of this unique book. According to Susan, this publication is a "worthwhile endeavor," and given "the League's focus on child advocacy," it is of great significance, "to produce a cookbook that promotes healthy lifestyle choices beginning at an early age." She looks forward to preparing many fun recipes with her grandchildren!

Erin Luetkemeier, a mother, community volunteer, and 2009–2010 President of The Junior League of New Orleans, Inc., sums up the importance of this worthy endeavor, sharing her pride in "being part of a project that addresses one of the largest health crises our country faces today—poor nutrition and obesity. I am proud of the training that I and other League volunteers received from research to publication. I am proud of all The Junior League of New Orleans, Inc., member volunteers, past, present, and future, that spend their precious time helping others and improving our community. It has been an honor to bring *Crescent City Moons, Dishes and Spoons* to children and families, including our own, for years to come."

On behalf of The Junior League of New Orleans, Inc., and *Crescent City Moons, Dishes and Spoons,* I wish you delicious and healthful recipes, family togetherness, and most of all—joy in the process. By purchasing *Crescent City Moons, Dishes and Spoons,* you help guarantee the continued success of The Junior League of New Orleans, Inc., in training volunteers, developing the potential of women, and improving our communities.

Leah Nunn Engelhardt
2008–2009 President, The Junior League of New Orleans, Inc.

Foreword

In the not-too-distant past, family meals were the norm rather than the exception.

When I was a youngster, my mother (and sometimes Papa) rose early in the morning to prepare a full breakfast before we went our respective separate ways to school and work. There were eggs, perhaps toast, biscuits or corn bread, ham, and sometimes creamy grits. Homemade jams, jellies, or fig preserves were passed around with butter that came not from the grocery store, but from my grandfather's farm. If we had cereal, it floated in milk that also came from Pop-Pete's cows at his farm.

More often than not, we were sent to school with our lunch box packed with sandwiches (tuna salad, ham and cheese, or sometimes leftover baked chicken), an apple or an orange, and maybe a cookie or two. At least once a week, usually on Friday, my siblings and I had permission to leave our small school campus to join our parents for lunch at a nearby café. Ah, then we could fill up on seafood gumbo, or fried catfish and potato salad, and a wedge of lemon pie made by the restaurant staff.

Supper was always a family affair. In fact, I could tell you what was for the evening meal simply by knowing the day of the week. For instance, Monday night was usually red beans (or white beans) cooked long and slow with the leftover ham bone from Sunday dinner. The creamy beans were served on a mound of rice (from our local fields), and there was always a salad of mixed greens and homegrown tomatoes when in season.

Tuesday night's fare was what we called "sticky chicken." A plump chicken was cut up into serving pieces (yep, bones and skin—can you imagine?) and smothered with lots of onions and bell peppers and served over the ubiquitous rice.

Wednesday night was "paper day" because Papa was the publisher and editor of our local newspaper, so we all reported after school to the "printing office" to help fold the newspapers by hand, then prepare them for mailing or bundle them up for delivery to the newsstands. Supper was ham sandwiches, eaten during a break from our work, made with ham hand-sliced by the owner of the grocery store, which was conveniently accessible behind our printing office.

Weekend meals were all about family.

My father was one of twelve children, and at his parents' home the stoves rarely got cold. There were platters of fried chicken, bowls of rice dressing, and in-season vegetables that included smothered okra, baked sweet potatoes, and lima beans.

If we had Sunday dinner with my mother's family, the Broussards, we enjoyed everything that came from their farm. A gumbo made with chicken and sausage (from the smokehouse on the farm) often began our meal. A plump, baked hen was ever present at the dinner table. Vegetables such as beans, turnips, corn, tomatoes, eggplant, and okra came straight from the garden located not far from the kitchen door.

Desserts at both houses were traditional south Louisiana fare—creamy bread pudding (made with day-old bread), gâteau de sirop (cake made with pure cane syrup), pecan pies (there were plenty of pecan trees on the property), and fig cake (we always had an abundance of Celeste fig trees).

Because our families were so close-knit, we had opportune time to interact with extended family—grandparents, parents, aunts, uncles, and many, many cousins. It was a joyous time since wherever we were, there were many outdoor activities to burn off all those calories.

These family gatherings offered great occasions to learn how to cook from whoever was in the kitchen. From my perch on a kitchen stool, I often watched Aunt Grace make a roux, shove a corn bread in the oven, and direct a helper to stir a pot of rice dressing—all with the greatest of ease.

I often spent Saturday afternoons with Tantes Belle and May helping them "put up" maque choux and okra or make preserves of fig and pears.

I realize times have changed, but mealtimes can still be family times. While both parents may have to work and children have busy schedules with school and extracurricular activities, it's important to MAKE TIME for a shared meal, even if it's only once or twice during the week, or a Saturday morning leisurely breakfast and for sure, a Sunday dinner.

Older children can be given kitchen tasks while younger ones can certainly help set the table. Allow the children, with a little help from the adults, to plan a menu.

Foreword continued

If they are allowed to participate in planning meals, they will be delighted with the results. Take children of all ages with you to the markets and introduce them to fresh produce, meats, and seafood. If there is a farmers' market in your area, take advantage of all the fresh ingredients available. Encourage children to try something new and by all means, avoid prepackaged, microwaveable products when possible.

Sure, it takes organization to bring nutritional meals to the table, but you will be amazed at the results. Teach children, at an early age, the importance of eating well. Pique their interest by showing them several preparations of food. For instance, chicken doesn't have to be fried to be good. It can be broiled, grilled, or baked and served with vegetables tossed with fresh herbs. Same goes for fish and other seafood. Desserts can be as simple as baked apples spiked with a sprinkling of brown sugar, cinnamon, and nutmeg and a drizzle of butter. An afternoon treat or a dessert made with in-season berries folded into plain yogurt flavored with snipped fresh mint and made crunchy with the addition of nuts is delicious.

And be aware that it's not so much what we eat, but the amount of it. In other words, "everything in moderation" has always been my motto.

Although we live in an electronic world, it's important that children of all ages be physically active. There is a time and a place for computers and all the games, for iPods, and television, but these activities should be limited. Get outdoors with your children and put some fresh air into their bodies. Plan family activities on the weekends—go canoeing, camping, biking, fishing, or hiking TOGETHER.

Cooking and eating should be fun, not a drudge. In the South, we are fortunate to have a culture where food is a way of life. It is an important part of our heritage, and we should all be responsible to help preserve it. It all begins with teaching our children to eat healthfully.

Marcelle Bienvenu
Cookbook Author, Food Columnist, Food Historian

Introduction

There's something magical that draws us into the kitchen. Whether at home with family or at a party with friends, the kitchen becomes the epicenter of the house. Fond memories take us back to childhood as the aromas invoke warm thoughts of meals enjoyed with loved ones.

Times have changed, however, and daily schedules are hectic. But, we should still try to make time for the simple things that bring everyone together at the end of the day: enjoying meals and conversations as a family.

Involving kids in the cooking process will not only help us put dinner on the table, it also will allow our families to spend more time together in the evenings.

There are so many different ways to get kids interested in helping out in the kitchen. Of course, the skill level will vary with age. Simple tasks that can be accomplished even by the youngest chefs include mashing potatoes, stirring the pots, peeling fruits or vegetables, and beating eggs. Older kids may enjoy tossing a salad, measuring ingredients, or grating cheese. Make it creative and fun, and you may be surprised when they want to learn more! Plus, as parents we can teach them the importance of eating healthfully while spending enjoyable time together.

Including children in the grocery shopping will give them a great sense of accomplishment as well as help them develop new skills. Allow children to select recipes that appeal to them and head out to the grocery store. Start in the produce section and let kids pick out their favorite fruits and vegetables. Encourage them to "eat a rainbow" and enjoy bright red, orange, purple, and green fruits and vegetables, challenging them to see how many different colors they can find. These antioxidant-rich fruits and vegetables are an important part of a nutritious diet, providing vitamins and minerals essential to growth as well as enhancing healthy eyes, skin, hair, and nails—overall, helping our bodies to function properly.

Introduction continued

Teach them how to choose nutrient-dense protein foods such as eggs, lean meats, peanut butter, nuts, beans, and soy products. Protein foods are also essential for growth as well as helping to build muscle and aid in our body's ability to heal. Other good sources of protein are low-fat dairy products such as milk, cheese, yogurt, and cottage cheese. Dairy foods provide protein as well as calcium for healthy bones and teeth.

Encourage heart-healthy fats that provide essential fatty acids in place of saturated and trans fats (one exception is children under two years of age, when saturated fat is crucial for brain development). Dietary fats are critical for hormone production and healthy hair, skin, and nails; they also aid the body in absorbing fat-soluble vitamins A, D, E, and K. Plus, including small amounts of fat helps to sustain energy levels during the day. Examples include nuts and seeds, avocado, nut butters such as peanut or almond butter, olive and canola oils, and omega-3–rich fish like salmon, halibut, and tuna.

Whole grains are yet another cornerstone of a healthy diet. Whole grains provide fiber, which promotes digestive health. Plus, fiber helps to sustain energy throughout the day. Examples include breads, cereals, oats, whole wheat pasta, and brown rice. Look for products that list whole grain as the first ingredient and contain at least three grams of fiber per serving.

Limit low-nutrient foods as much as possible. It is often difficult for children to resist foods like chips, cookies, sodas, and candy when these items are around the house, and it suppresses their appetites when the dinner bell rings. Make every effort to keep healthful snacks readily available. Encouraging them to make better choices will help build healthier habits throughout life.

Each meal should include sources of foods from all of these food groups. A combination of protein, fiber-rich carbohydrates, fruits and vegetables, and unsaturated fats will give kids the essentials they need to focus in school and provide energy, in addition to supplying vital nutrients to support optimal growth. A balanced diet is critical at all stages of growth and development for children. It also helps prevent obesity and weight-related diseases such as heart disease, diabetes, and high blood pressure. As parents, we are their prime example, and the habits they develop in their youth will be the ones they will have for a lifetime.

Remember, creating a warm mealtime environment at home not only nourishes the body but also nourishes the soul. This is a special time when your children will create their own memories of growing up and enjoy being part of creating meals to share with family and friends.

Elesha Kelleher

Elesha Kelleher, R.D./L.D.N., MPH
Nutritionist at Ochsner's Elmwood Fitness Center

Crescent City Coos

The first few months of having a newborn can be daunting even for the most well-intentioned, conscientious parents. After all, this is the time we begin to lay the foundation for a healthy life, and we want to be sure babies are getting everything they need.

Infants up to four to six months of age will receive all the nutrients they require through breast milk and/or formula. At four to six months, you can begin adding more nutrients, ideally at a rate of one new soft food per month. Cereals, then fruits and vegetables should be introduced, followed by puréed meats.

Daily caloric intake for children ages one to three years should be approximately 900 to 1,000 calories. Daily nutrient intake starting at age one should include the following: one to two ounces of lean protein, two to three ounces of whole grains, one cup of fruit, three-fourths to one cup of vegetables, and two cups of milk.

In this stage of development, children are asserting their independence as well as developing food preferences they may carry through life. This presents an opportunity for parents to broaden their children's palates and provide them with healthy food choices. Parents control the types of foods that are available and children decide what and how much to eat. Remember, children are naturally able to gauge when they are hungry and when they are full.

Tofu Cheerios Snack

14 ounces firm tofu, drained and cut into cubes

1 1/2 cups crushed Cheerios

Nutritional Profiles 230–233

1 Coat the tofu cubes with the crushed Cheerios. Serve as a snack.

Yield: 4 (3-ounce) servings

It doesn't have to be stressful figuring out what foods babies will eat. Always check first with your pediatrician before introducing new foods. Once you get the green light, serve a variety of foods until you get to know your baby's preferences. **A Crescent City Baby Coos:** "I like whatever you're having as long as you cut it up small enough for me to chew."
—Beau Bregman

Baby Beau's
Butternut Squash Soup

½ small onion, chopped

1 teaspoon olive oil

1 cup homemade chicken stock (page 207)

8 ounces butternut squash, chopped

1 pear, peeled and chopped

2 ounces celery, finely chopped

½ cup milk

Pinch of chopped fresh thyme

Pinch of oregano

Freshly ground pepper to taste

Nutritional Profiles 230–233

1 Sauté the onion in the olive oil in a saucepan over medium heat until the onion is golden brown. Stir in the stock.

2 Add the squash, pear and celery and bring to a rolling boil. Reduce the heat to low.

3 Simmer for 10 minutes, stirring occasionally. Stir in the milk, thyme, oregano and pepper. Simmer just until the vegetables are tender. Let stand until cool and serve.

Yield: 6 (½-cup) servings

The seeds of the butternut squash are edible and make a nutritious snack for older children and grown-ups. Rinse the seeds under warm water to remove the fibrous material and pat dry with a paper towel. Toss the seeds with some olive oil in a bowl and spread in a single layer on a baking sheet. Roast in a preheated 325-degree oven until dry and crisp. Season with salt, if desired.

Banana Avocado Baby Food

The trick is to mix roughly the same amount of each ingredient.

¹/3 banana

¹/3 small avocado

3 tablespoons plain or
vanilla yogurt

1 Mash the banana, avocado and yogurt in a bowl until
smooth. Serve immediately.

Yield: 1 (1-cup) serving

Nutritional Profiles 230–233

Fruit Salad

¹/2 avocado, chopped

¹/2 small banana, sliced

¹/2 papaya, chopped

¹/2 kiwifruit, sliced

2 ounces plain yogurt

Drop of pure maple syrup

1 Combine the avocado, banana, papaya and kiwifruit in a
bowl and mix gently. If this is being served to a young baby,
purée the fruit.

2 Top the fruit mixture with the yogurt and drizzle with the
maple syrup.

Yield: 4 (¹/2-cup) servings

Nutritional Profiles 230–233

Tropical Fruit Treat

This recipe will yield quite a few portions, and it has a lovely, unusual flavor.

1 butternut squash

2 pears

1 papaya, chopped

1 avocado, chopped

Nutritional Profiles 230–233

1   Peel and chop the squash, discarding the seeds. Steam the squash in a steamer over simmering water until tender. Remove the squash to a bowl using a slotted spoon, reserving the cooking liquid.

2   Peel the pears and remove the cores; slice the pears. Simmer in a steamer over simmering water for 10 minutes; drain.

3   Process the squash, pears, papaya and avocado in a blender until puréed, adding the reserved cooking liquid as needed for the desired consistency.

Yield: 6 (1/2-cup) servings

As your baby gets a little older, thicken the consistency of these baby first-food recipes by omitting some of the liquids. Once your baby is able to eat solid foods, you can introduce exciting new elements to your baby's diet, including a wide variety of fruits and vegetables.

Beef Stroganoff

¹/2 cup egg noodles

I cup chopped filet mignon or beef tenderloin

Pinch of paprika

Pepper to taste

2 teaspoons olive oil

5 button mushrooms, sliced

I tablespoon chopped onion

3 cups low-sodium organic chicken stock

I teaspoon finely chopped parsley

Nutritional Profiles 230–233

1 Cook the noodles in boiling water in a saucepan until tender; drain. Season the beef with paprika and pepper.

2 Sauté the beef in the olive oil in a large deep skillet until the beef begins to brown. Stir in the mushrooms, onion, I tablespoon of the stock and the parsley.

3 Sauté for 3 minutes. Add the remaining stock and mix well. Reduce the heat and simmer, covered, for 25 minutes. Reserve ¹/2 cup of the pan juices.

4 Combine the remaining beef mixture and noodles in a food processor or blender. Process to the desired consistency, gradually adding the reserved pan juices as needed.

Yield: 8 (¹/2-cup) servings

Chicken Noodle Delight

2 cups water

1/2 cup egg noodles

1/4 cup chopped baby carrots

1/4 cup chopped celery

1 tablespoon minced onion

1 teaspoon olive oil

1/2 teaspoon salt

1/8 teaspoon pepper

1 sprig of thyme, finely chopped

1/2 cup chopped cooked chicken breast or thigh

1/2 cup low-sodium organic chicken stock

1 bay leaf

1 Bring the water to a boil in a saucepan and add the noodles. Boil for 10 minutes or until tender; drain.

2 Sauté the carrots, celery and onion in the olive oil in a saucepan until the vegetables are tender. Stir in the salt, pepper and thyme.

3 Cook for 2 minutes. Add the chicken, stock and bay leaf and mix well.

4 Simmer for 10 minutes. Discard the bay leaf. Combine the noodles and chicken mixture in a food processor or blender and process until smooth.

5 Add additional stock for a creamier consistency or dry rice cereal for a thicker consistency.

Yield: 4 (1/2-cup) servings

Nutritional Profiles 230–233

Chicken and Squash Dinner

2 ounces cooked butternut squash

1 ounce cooked chicken

2 tablespoons cooked brown rice

1 tablespoon shredded
Cheddar cheese

Nutritional Profiles 230–233

1 Process the squash, chicken, rice and cheese in a food processor or blender until puréed.

2 Add breast milk or formula for a thinner consistency, if desired. You may mash the ingredients in a bowl.

Yield: 1 (1/2-cup) serving

Turkey Orzo

1 cup orzo

8 ounces ground turkey

1 zucchini, chopped

1 yellow squash, chopped

1 carrot, chopped

1 (14-ounce) can
crushed tomatoes

1/2 cup (2 ounces) grated
Parmesan cheese

Nutritional Profiles 230–233

1 Cook the pasta using the package directions; drain. Brown the turkey in a skillet, stirring until crumbly; drain. Stir in the zucchini, yellow squash and carrot.

2 Cook for 5 minutes. Stir in the tomatoes and cook for 5 minutes.

3 Process the turkey mixture in a food processor until minced. Mix the turkey mixture and pasta in a bowl until combined and sprinkle with the cheese.

Yield: 6 (3/4-cup) servings

Photograph for this recipe on page 28.

Salmon Spinach and Peas

1 tablespoon chopped onion

1 teaspoon olive oil

1 (4-ounce) salmon fillet

1 1/2 cups low-sodium organic chicken stock

1 1/2 cups water

1/2 cup frozen peas

1/2 cup frozen spinach, thawed

Nutritional Profiles 230–233

1 Sauté the onion in the olive oil in a skillet until the onion is tender. Add the salmon to the skillet and cook for 4 minutes per side. Stir in the stock, water, peas and spinach.

2 Simmer for 15 minutes, stirring occasionally. Remove the solids to a food processor using a slotted spoon, reserving the cooking liquid.

3 Process the solids in the food processor, gradually adding the reserved liquid as needed for the desired consistency.

Yield: 4 (1/2-cup) servings

Quesadillas

1 small pear, peeled and cored

1 (12-inch) whole wheat tortilla

2 tablespoons shredded mozzarella cheese or other mild cheese

Nutritional Profiles 230–233

1 Wrap the pear in foil and place on a baking sheet. Bake in a preheated 350-degree oven until the pear is tender. Let stand until cool. Mash the pear in a bowl until smooth. Spread over half the tortilla and sprinkle with the cheese. Fold the tortilla over to enclose the filling, forming a semicircle.

2 Arrange the quesadilla in a preheated skillet. Cook for several minutes or until the cheese melts. Cut into wedges. Serve when cooled to a safe temperature.

Yield: 2 (1/2-tortilla) servings

Photograph for this recipe on page 28.

Ga-Ga Guacamole

I avocado

I tablespoon tomato juice

Chopped fresh cilantro to taste

Ground cumin to taste

1 Peel the avocado and place in a bowl. Mash the avocado until smooth.

2 Stir in the tomato juice, cilantro and cumin. Serve as a side dish or dip.

Yield: 4 ($1/4$-cup) servings

Nutritional Profiles 230–233

Pumpkin Spinach Pasta

2 lasagna noodles

I cup chopped pumpkin

I teaspoon olive oil

$1/2$ cup low-sodium organic chicken stock

$1/4$ cup drained thawed frozen spinach

I sage leaf, finely chopped (optional)

Dash of pepper

1 Bring a small saucepan of water to a boil and add the pasta. Cook for 10 minutes or until the pasta is tender; drain.

2 Sauté the pumpkin in the olive oil in a skillet over medium heat until the pumpkin is softened and beginning to brown. Stir in the stock, spinach, sage and pepper. Simmer for 20 minutes or until the pumpkin is fork-tender.

3 Combine the pasta and pumpkin mixture in a food processor or blender. Process until smooth, adding additional warm chicken stock for a creamier consistency or dry rice cereal for a thicker consistency.

Yield: 4 ($1/2$-cup) servings

Nutritional Profiles 230–233

Cauliflower Lasagna

3 lasagna noodles

I cup chopped cauliflower

6 ounces tomato sauce

1/4 teaspoon each finely chopped fresh oregano and fresh basil

Dash of pepper

Pinch of garlic powder

Nutritional Profiles 230–233

1 Bring a small saucepan of water to a boil and add the pasta. Cook for 10 minutes or until the pasta is tender; drain.

2 Combine the cauliflower, tomato sauce, oregano, basil, pepper and garlic powder in a saucepan and mix well. Simmer, covered, for 15 minutes, stirring occasionally.

3 Combine the pasta and cauliflower mixture in a food processor or blender. Process until smooth, adding warm chicken stock for a creamier consistency or dry rice cereal for a thicker consistency.

Yield: 8 (1/2-cup) servings

Popeye Pasta

4 ounces miniature pasta shells

1/2 cup frozen spinach, thawed

1/4 garlic clove (optional)

Olive oil (optional)

2 tablespoons butter

1/2 cup milk

1/2 cup (2 ounces) grated Parmesan cheese

Nutritional Profiles 230–233

1 Cook the pasta in boiling water in a saucepan using the package directions; drain. Cook a few minutes longer if you need to mash the pasta. Simmer the spinach and garlic in olive oil in a skillet, if desired. Pulse the spinach mixture in a food processor.

2 Melt the butter in a saucepan and stir in the milk. Cook over low heat for 2 minutes. Stir in the pasta and spinach mixture. Pulse in a food processor to the desired consistency at this point if preparing for young babies. Stir in the cheese. Add additional milk when reheating to prevent lumps.

Yield: 6 (1/2-cup) servings

Rosemary Potatoes

4 small red potatoes, cut into
1-inch pieces

1/2 sprig of rosemary, minced

2 teaspoons olive oil

3/4 cup low-sodium organic
chicken stock

Dash of pepper

1 Sauté the potatoes and rosemary in the olive oil in a saucepan over medium-low heat just until the potatoes begin to brown. Add the stock and pepper and simmer for 15 minutes or until the potatoes are tender, stirring occasionally.

2 Process the potato mixture in a blender until smooth, adding additional stock for a creamier consistency or rice cereal for a thicker consistency.

Yield: 2 (1/2-cup) servings

Squash and Fruit Purée

1 ounce dried apricots

1 ounce raisins

4 ounces cooked butternut squash

1/2 ripe pear, peeled and cored

Pinch of cinnamon

1 tablespoon wheat germ

1 Combine the apricots and raisins with enough warm water to cover in a bowl. Plump for 30 minutes; drain.

2 Process the apricots, raisins, squash, pear and cinnamon in a food processor until puréed or mash the ingredients in a bowl. Sprinkle each serving with 1 1/2 teaspoons of the wheat germ.

Yield: 2 (1/2-cup) servings

Ratatouille

5 button mushrooms, sliced

1 tablespoon chopped onion

1 teaspoon olive oil

1 yellow squash, sliced

1 zucchini, sliced

1 red bell pepper, chopped

$1/2$ cup low-sodium organic chicken stock

$1/2$ cup water

5 grape tomatoes, chopped

$1/4$ cup frozen spinach, thawed

1 basil leaf, chopped

Nutritional Profiles 230–233

1 Sauté the mushrooms and onion in the olive oil in a saucepan until tender. Add the yellow squash, zucchini and bell pepper and mix well.

2 Simmer for 4 minutes; stir in the stock, water, tomatoes, spinach and basil.

3 Simmer for 10 minutes. Strain the squash mixture, reserving the solids and the liquid separately. Process the reserved solids in a food processor, gradually adding the reserved liquid as needed for the desired consistency.

Yield: 4 ($1/2$-cup) servings

Remember to consult your child's pediatrician before introducing any new foods to your baby. Always wait four days after introducing a new food. This will help you identify any food that may cause allergic reactions or digestive problems in your baby.

Green Vegetable Medley

I tablespoon chopped onion

I teaspoon olive oil

I zucchini, sliced

I asparagus spear, sliced

I cup low-sodium organic chicken stock

I cup water

$^1/_2$ cup peas

$^1/_2$ cup chopped broccoli

$^1/_2$ cup green beans

$^1/_2$ cup frozen spinach, thawed

Nutritional Profiles 230–233

1 Sauté the onion in the olive oil in a saucepan until the onion is almost tender. Add the zucchini and asparagus and sauté for 4 minutes.

2 Stir in the stock, water, peas, broccoli, beans and spinach. Simmer, partially covered, for 20 minutes. Drain, reserving the solids and the liquid separately.

3 Process the reserved solids in a food processor, gradually adding the reserved liquid as needed for the desired consistency.

Yield: 6 ($^1/_2$-cup) servings

Photograph for this recipe on page 28.

Yellow Vegetable Medley

1/2 butternut squash

I teaspoon olive oil

5 baby carrots, sliced

1/2 orange bell pepper, chopped

I teaspoon olive oil

1/2 cup chopped pumpkin

I sweet potato, chopped

I cup low-sodium organic chicken stock

I cup water

Nutritional Profiles 230–233

1 Brush the cut side of the squash with I teaspoon olive oil and arrange the squash cut side down in a baking dish. Bake in a preheated 400-degree oven for 45 minutes.

2 Sauté the carrots and bell pepper in I teaspoon olive oil in a skillet for 4 minutes. Add the pumpkin and sweet potato and sauté just until the sweet potato begins to brown. Stir in the stock and water. Simmer, partially covered, for 20 minutes or until the sweet potato is tender.

3 Scrape the squash pulp into a food processor. Drain the carrot mixture, reserving the solids and the liquid separately. Add the reserved solids to the food processor and process to the desired consistency, gradually adding the reserved liquid as needed.

Yield: 6 (1/2-cup) servings

Photograph for this recipe on page 28.

Butternut squash is NOT a common allergen and is rarely the cause of any allergic reactions in babies. It is also easy to digest.

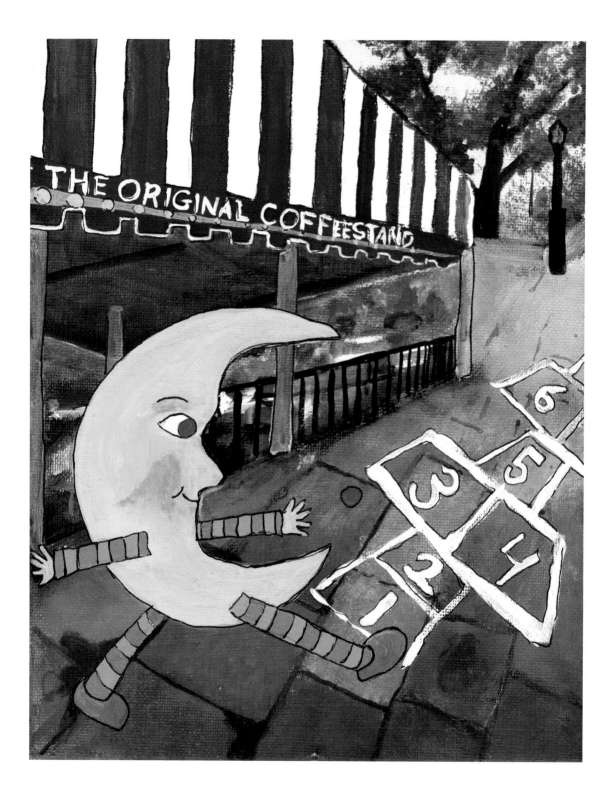

Crescent City Cuties

The toddler and school-age years are a time of remarkable physical and mental growth. Consequently, it is also a time when good nutrition is essential. This can be a frustrating time for even the most diligent parents because young children are developing strong food preferences, making it sometimes difficult to provide a variety of vital nutrients.

You may need to introduce a new food as many as eight to fifteen times for children to acquire new tastes. Try introducing a new food along with an old favorite. Forcing children to clean their plates may cause negative feelings about mealtime.

Know that children's caloric intake will vary from day to day. Young tummies are little, so younger children may benefit from four to six miniature meals per day. This will maximize energy levels and allow for a variety of nutrients to be offered in smaller amounts.

Daily caloric intake for children ages four to thirteen ranges from 1,200 to 1,600 calories for females, and from 1,400 to 1,800 calories for males. Daily nutrient intake should include the following: three to five ounces of meat, four to six ounces of grains, one and one-half cups of fruit, one to two cups of vegetables, and two to three cups of milk.

Remember, kids at this age are watching your behaviors, so be sure you are setting a good example.

Orange Julius

Children love this beverage. Serve it in small, clear juice glasses because it looks inviting and juice glasses are the perfect size for little ones.

2 cups fresh orange juice

I cup milk

$^1/_4$ cup sugar

I teaspoon vanilla extract

5 or 6 ice cubes

1 Combine the orange juice, milk, sugar, vanilla and ice cubes in a blender. Process for 30 seconds and pour into juice glasses.

Yield: 6 ($^1/_2$-cup) servings

Photograph for this recipe on page 54.

Nutritional Profiles 230–233

Strawberry Princess Punch

4 ounces frozen strawberries

I cup sugar

14 ounces pineapple juice

4 (6-ounce) cans frozen lemonade concentrate

16 ounces club soda

16 ounces ginger ale

1 Thaw the strawberries, retaining the juices. Combine the undrained strawberries, sugar, pineapple juice, lemonade concentrate, club soda and ginger ale in a large punch bowl and stir gently to combine. Ladle into punch cups.

Yield: 16 (1-cup) servings

Nutritional Profiles 230–233

Gourmet Granola

Tasty, popular, and nutritious snack. Take to sports events, school events, camping trips, or slumber parties.

2 cups rolled oats

I cup sunflower seeds

$1/2$ cup chopped walnuts or pecans

$1/2$ cup slivered almonds

$1/2$ cup shredded coconut

$1/4$ cup vegetable oil

$3/4$ cup honey

$1/2$ cup raisins

1 Toss the oats, sunflower seeds, walnuts, almonds and coconut in a bowl. Whisk the oil and honey in a bowl until blended and add to the oats mixture. Stir until combined.

2 Spread the oats mixture on an 11×15-inch baking sheet sprayed with nonstick cooking spray. Bake in a preheated 300-degree oven for 30 minutes or until golden brown, stirring occasionally.

3 Let stand until cool; fold in the raisins. Store in an airtight container.

Yield: 12 ($1/2$-cup) servings

Nutritional Profiles 230–233

Quick Kabobs

¹/2 cup sliced banana

¹/2 cup apple chunks

¹/2 cup melon chunks
(watermelon, cantaloupe,
honeydew and/or kiwifruit)

¹/2 cup Cheddar cheese cubes

¹/2 cup orange juice

¹/2 cup shredded coconut

Nutritional Profiles 230–233

1 Alternate the banana, apple, melon and cheese equally on eight skewers. Dip the kabobs in the orange juice and coat with the coconut.

2 Use other fruits such as pineapple chunks, cherry halves and/or grapes as desired. Coat with sesame seeds and/or flax seeds for variety.

Yield: 8 kabobs

Photograph for this recipe on page 54.

Sam's Strawberry Sandwiches

I loaf French bread

8 ounces cream cheese, softened

I pound strawberries, sliced

I tablespoon honey

Nutritional Profiles 230–233

1 Cut the bread loaf horizontally into halves. Spread the cream cheese over the cut side of the bottom half. Arrange the strawberry slices over the cream cheese and drizzle with the honey.

2 Top with the remaining bread half cut side down. Cut into twelve equal sandwiches.

Yield: 12 servings

Tutti-Frutti Tacos

2 (6-inch) corn tortillas

2 tablespoons peanut butter

1 cup chopped mixed fresh fruit
(use kiwifruit, pineapple,
banana, mango, strawberries
and blueberries)

1 tablespoon shredded coconut

Nutritional Profiles 230–233

1 Microwave the tortillas for 10 seconds or until warm. Spread each warm tortilla with 1 tablespoon of the peanut butter.

2 Sprinkle each with half the fruit and half the coconut. Fold over to enclose the filling and serve.

Yield: 2 servings

Choosing the freshest ingredients possible is always a good rule of thumb when preparing delicious and healthful foods. Visit different grocery stores, shops, or vendors to determine where the best selections can be found. **A fresh food tip from a Crescent City Cutie:** *"My favorite healthy food is strawberries. You grow it in a garden and when it's ready you pick them and you eat them."*

—Madeline "Molly" Robert

Dill Pickle Soup

*This is a very hearty dish and is usually served as a meal,
especially during the colder months.*

1 pound bacon

7 quarts water

10 beef bouillon cubes

8 large potatoes, peeled and cut
into large chunks

1 (24-ounce) jar kosher dill pickles

3 cups sour cream

Salt and pepper to taste

Dill weed to taste

Nutritional Profiles 230–233

1 Arrange the bacon in a single layer on a baking sheet with sides and bake in a preheated oven using the package directions. The object of baking the bacon versus frying is to make sure the bacon is soft, not crispy. Drain the bacon on paper towels. Let cool slightly and tear into bite-size pieces.

2 Bring the water to a boil in a stockpot and add the bouillon cubes. Add the potatoes and boil until the potatoes are tender. Drain, reserving 3 to 4 cups of the broth. Return the potatoes to the stockpot; the potatoes will be very wet. Beat the potatoes until puréed to the consistency of soupy mashed potatoes. Add the reserved broth until the consistency of a thick soup and mix well. Stir in the bacon.

3 Drain the pickles, reserving the juice. Chop the pickles into bite-size pieces and add to the soup. Stir in the sour cream. Add the desired amount of the reserved pickle juice and desired amount of the remaining broth to the soup until the desired consistency. Be careful not to add too much pickle juice. Season with salt, pepper and dill weed. Simmer just until heated through. Ladle into soup bowls and serve warm with French bread.

4 The individual flavors of the potatoes, sour cream, bacon and dill weed should be distinctly present. Rule of thumb when preparing this soup is use more salt and less pepper, more broth and less pickle juice and dill weed. The soup is better thicker than thin.

Yield: 24 (1-cup) servings

Pepper Boat Salads

This makes a hearty side dish for burgers and grilled chicken.
Mix and match red, yellow, and orange bell peppers for a fall display, or mix
red and green bell peppers for the Christmas season.

4 bell peppers

1 pint cherry tomatoes,
cut into quarters

1/2 cup low-fat sour cream

2 tablespoons chopped
green onions

1 tablespoon lemon juice

1/4 teaspoon salt

1/2 cup (2 ounces) shredded
Cheddar cheese

1 Slice the bell peppers lengthwise into halves. Discard the seeds and white membranes and rinse.

2 Combine the tomatoes, sour cream, green onions, lemon juice, salt and cheese in a bowl and mix well. Fill the bell pepper halves equally with the tomato mixture.

Yield: 8 servings

Photograph for this recipe on page 54.

Nutritional Profiles 230–233

Eat a variety of fresh vegetables every day. You can be creative with the way you mix and match food. **A creative cooking tip from a Crescent City Cutie:** *"Salad is the perfect meal because you can put cheese in it, dressing on it, chicken in it, and it still counts as a vegetable."*

—*Grayson Scott*

Beefy Noodles

1 (10-ounce) package frozen chopped spinach

1 (16-ounce) can spaghetti sauce with mushrooms

1 (8-ounce) can tomato sauce

1 (6-ounce) can tomato paste

1/2 teaspoon salt

Dash of pepper

1 pound ground beef

1 onion, chopped

1 garlic clove, minced

1 tablespoon vegetable oil

7 ounces shell macaroni, cooked and drained

1 cup (4 ounces) shredded sharp American cheese

1/2 cup soft bread crumbs

2 eggs, beaten

1/4 cup vegetable oil

Nutritional Profiles 230–233

1 Cook the spinach using the package directions. Drain, reserving the liquid. Press any excess moisture from the spinach into a measuring cup. Add enough water to the reserved spinach liquid to measure 1 cup.

2 Combine 1 cup spinach liquid, the spaghetti sauce, tomato sauce, tomato paste, salt and pepper in a bowl and mix well.

3 Brown the ground beef, onion and garlic in 1 tablespoon oil in a large skillet, stirring until the ground beef is crumbly; drain. Stir in the spaghetti sauce mixture and simmer for 10 minutes.

4 Mix the spinach, pasta, cheese, bread crumbs, eggs and 1/4 cup oil in a bowl. Spread the spinach mixture in a 9×13-inch baking dish and top with the ground beef mixture.

5 Bake in a preheated 350-degree oven for 30 minutes. Let stand for 10 minutes before serving.

Yield: 10 servings

Marguerite's Meatballs

This recipe was created because the garlic and onions used in most meatballs are not palatable to many kids. The spinach is hardly detected.

1 (10-ounce) package frozen chopped spinach, thawed and drained

2 slices whole wheat bread

1 pound lean ground beef

2 eggs, lightly beaten

2 tablespoons chopped parsley

Salt and pepper to taste

1 tablespoon olive oil

1 (16-ounce) can tomato sauce

Nutritional Profiles 230–233

1 Press any excess moisture from the spinach. Soak the bread slices in water in a bowl until saturated. Drain the bread and squeeze dry.

2 Combine the spinach, bread, ground beef, eggs, parsley, salt and pepper in a bowl and mix well. Shape into meatballs about the size of golf balls.

3 Brown the meatballs in the olive oil in a skillet; drain. Arrange the meatballs in a single layer in a 3- or 4-quart baking dish. Pour the tomato sauce over the top.

4 Bake in a preheated 350-degree oven for 20 minutes or until heated through. Serve with hot cooked pasta.

Yield: 6 servings

Kids' Favorite Meat Loaf

1 1/2 pounds lean ground beef

2/3 cup evaporated milk

1/2 cup cracker crumbs

1 egg, beaten

1 tablespoon Worcestershire sauce

1 1/2 teaspoons salt

1 teaspoon dry mustard

1 teaspoon minced onion

1/4 teaspoon pepper

Nutritional Profiles 230–233

1 Combine the ground beef, evaporated milk, cracker crumbs and egg in a bowl and mix well. Add the Worcestershire sauce, salt, dry mustard, onion and pepper and mix well.

2 Shape the ground beef mixture into a loaf in a 5×9-inch loaf pan. Bake in a preheated 350-degree oven for 1 hour.

3 Let stand for 5 minutes before slicing. Great as leftovers or on a sandwich the next day.

Yield: 6 servings

When cooking with smaller children set expectations up front. Keep safety in mind. Clearly outline the jobs they can do and the ones that only an adult can do. **A Crescent City Cutie describes her favorite kitchen assignment:** *"I like to break the eggs and then whip them in the bowl with mommy's big fork. My favorite job is getting my stool to the kitchen so I can see over the countertops."*
—Avery Donnelly

Homemade Sloppy Joes

1 pound ground beef

1/2 cup finely chopped onion

1 cup ketchup

1/2 cup water

1/4 cup packed brown sugar

1 tablespoon white wine vinegar

1 tablespoon mustard

6 hamburger buns

Nutritional Profiles 230–233

1 Brown the ground beef with the onion in a skillet, stirring until the ground beef is crumbly; drain.

2 Whisk the ketchup, water, brown sugar, vinegar and mustard in a bowl until combined. Stir into the ground beef mixture.

3 Simmer over low heat for 5 to 10 minutes or until the flavors marry, stirring occasionally. Serve on hamburger buns.

Yield: 6 servings

Oven-Baked Barbecue Ribs

1 rack pork ribs

1 tablespoon McCormick
Season-All seasoned salt

1 (16-ounce) bottle
barbecue sauce

Nutritional Profiles 230–233

1 Rinse the ribs and pat dry. Rub the ribs with the seasoned salt. Drizzle a thin line of barbecue sauce down the center of the ribs. Wrap the ribs in foil.

2 Bake in a preheated 250-degree oven for 4 to 5 hours or until the meat is falling off the bones.

Yield: 6 servings

Noodles and Ham

1 cup frozen petite peas

12 ounces noodles

1 cup chopped cooked ham or
Canadian bacon

1 cup heavy cream or half-and-half

1 bunch green onions, chopped

Nutritional Profiles 230–233

1 Place the peas in a colander. Cook the noodles in a large saucepan using the package directions. Drain the noodles over the peas to slightly thaw the peas.

2 Return the noodle mixture to the saucepan and stir in the ham, cream and green onions. Simmer just until heated through. Serve with grated Parmesan cheese, hot Sister Schubert rolls and sliced fresh peaches.

3 You can sauté the ham in butter and heat the cream in the microwave before combining with the noodle mixture, if desired.

Yield: 6 servings

Ham Biscuits

1 pound ground ham

1/3 pound Swiss cheese or
Cheddar cheese, shredded

1 small onion, grated

1 teaspoon Worcestershire sauce

3 tablespoons poppy seeds

1 tablespoon mustard

1 1/2 cups (3 sticks)
butter, softened

3 packages small dinner rolls

Nutritional Profiles 230–233

1 Combine the ham, cheese, onion and Worcestershire sauce in a bowl and mix well. Mix the poppy seeds, mustard and butter in a bowl.

2 Split each package of rolls horizontally into two layers, leaving the bottom layers in the pans.

3 Spread the cut sides of the rolls with the butter mixture. Spread the ham mixture over the bottom layers of rolls. Top with remaining roll layers and cover with foil.

4 Bake in a preheated 400-degree oven for 10 to 15 minutes or until heated through.

5 You may bake at 300 degrees, increasing the baking time. Freeze before baking for future use, if desired.

Yield: 36 biscuits

Muffuletta Pasta

16 ounces penne

8 ounces Genoa salami, cut into chunks

8 ounces Smithfield ham, cut into chunks

8 ounces provolone cheese, cut into chunks

1 (16-ounce) jar Boscoli Italian olive salad

6 ounces Romano cheese, grated

1 (4-ounce) can sliced black olives

2 tablespoons olive-oil-packed chopped garlic

1 package shredded mozzarella cheese (optional)

Nutritional Profiles 230–233

1 Cook the pasta using the package directions; drain. Combine the pasta, salami, ham, provolone cheese, undrained olive salad, Romano cheese, black olives and garlic in a bowl and mix well.

2 Spoon the pasta mixture into a 9×13-inch baking dish and sprinkle with the mozzarella cheese.

3 Bake in a preheated 350-degree oven for 30 minutes or until the cheese melts.

4 Freeze before baking for future use, if desired. Remove from the freezer and bake using the directions given above.

Yield: 12 servings

Chicken Nuggets

Children can prepare the nuggets themselves. Make an assembly line starting with the chicken, proceeding to the butter, then to the bread crumb mixture, and then to the baking sheet. Or the nuggets can be coated with the butter all at once and tossed with the bread crumb mixture in a sealable plastic bag.

Chicken Nuggets

1 1/2 pounds chicken breasts or chicken strips

1/2 cup (1 stick) butter, melted

Italian-Style Chicken Nuggets

1 cup Italian-style bread crumbs

1/4 cup (1 ounce) grated Parmesan cheese

1 teaspoon paprika

Coconut Chicken Nuggets

1 cup unseasoned bread crumbs

1/2 cup shredded coconut

1/2 teaspoon cayenne pepper

1/2 teaspoon salt

Nutritional Profiles 230–233

1 For the nuggets, cut the chicken breasts into 1 1/2-inch cubes and dip in the butter. Proceed using one of the following variations.

2 For the Italian-style nuggets, mix the bread crumbs, cheese and paprika in a shallow dish. Coat the nuggets with the bread crumb mixture. Line a baking sheet with foil and spray with nonstick cooking spray.

3 For the coconut nuggets, mix the bread crumbs, coconut, cayenne pepper and salt in a shallow dish. Coat the nuggets with the bread crumb mixture. Line a baking sheet with foil and spray with nonstick cooking spray.

4 Arrange the nuggets in a single layer on the prepared baking sheet. Bake in a preheated 400-degree oven for 25 minutes or until golden brown, turning once. Serve with Honey Mustard Dipping Sauce on page 52.

Yield: 4 servings

Photograph for this recipe on page 54.

Honey Mustard Dipping Sauce

½ cup Dijon mustard or
yellow mustard

¼ cup honey

2 tablespoons apple cider vinegar

1 teaspoon lemon juice

Dash of cayenne pepper

1 Combine the Dijon mustard, honey, vinegar, lemon juice and cayenne pepper in a saucepan and mix well.

2 Heat for about 4 minutes, stirring constantly until the honey dissolves.

Yield: 4 (2-ounce) servings

Nutritional Profiles 230–233

Chicken Poppy Seed

1 pound chicken, boiled

1 (10-ounce) can reduced-fat
cream of chicken soup

2 cups low-fat sour cream

3 tablespoons poppy seeds

1 sleeve Ritz crackers,
finely crushed

2 tablespoons butter, melted

1 Cut the chicken into bite-size pieces. Combine the chicken, soup, sour cream and poppy seeds in a bowl and mix well.

2 Place the cracker crumbs and butter in a bowl and toss to coat.

3 Spread the chicken mixture in a baking dish sprayed with nonstick cooking spray and sprinkle with the cracker crumbs.

4 Bake in a preheated 350-degree oven for 35 to 40 minutes or until golden brown.

Yield: 6 servings

Nutritional Profiles 230–233

Children's Fried Rice

Add peas, carrots, or vegetables of choice for variety and added nutrition.

1 cup brown rice

1 (16-ounce) can low-sodium chicken broth

4 (4-ounce) boneless skinless chicken breasts, cut into bite-size pieces

1 egg

3 tablespoons milk

Nutritional Profiles 230–233

1 Bring the rice and broth to a boil in a saucepan; reduce the heat. Cook until the rice is tender; drain.

2 Sauté the chicken in a nonstick skillet over low to medium heat until cooked through, turning occasionally.

3 Whisk the egg and milk in a bowl until blended. Scramble the egg mixture in a skillet sprayed with nonstick cooking spray until the desired degree of doneness.

4 Combine the rice, chicken and scrambled egg in a skillet. Cook over low heat just until brown, stirring frequently. Cool slightly and garnish with parsley and carrot strips.

Yield: 4 servings

Photograph for this recipe on page 54.

Kid-Friendly Easy Chili

1 pound ground turkey

2 tablespoons olive oil

1 cup chopped onion

1 (15-ounce) can pinto beans

1 (15-ounce) can black beans

1 (16-ounce) can beef broth

1 (10-ounce) can Ro-Tel tomatoes

1 1/2 teaspoons chili powder

1 teaspoon chopped garlic

1/2 teaspoon cayenne pepper, or to taste

Salt and black pepper to taste

Nutritional Profiles 230–233

1 Brown the ground turkey in the olive oil in a saucepan for 5 to 10 minutes. Stir in the onion and cook until the onion is tender.

2 Add the beans, broth, tomatoes, chili powder, garlic, cayenne pepper, salt and black pepper to the ground turkey mixture and mix well.

3 Cook until the chili is heated through and the desired consistency, stirring occasionally. Ladle into chili bowls.

4 For Spicy Frito Pie, spoon the chili over Fritos and sprinkle with shredded Cheddar cheese.

Yield: 8 (1-cup) servings

Yummy Tuna Casserole

1 package Kraft Deluxe macaroni
and cheese

1 (6-ounce) can white
tuna, drained

3/4 (10-ounce) can diced tomatoes
or Ro-Tel tomatoes

1/2 cup (2 ounces) grated
Parmesan cheese

Nutritional Profiles 230–233

1 Prepare the macaroni and cheese in a saucepan using the package directions. Stir in the tuna and tomatoes.

2 Cook for 5 to 7 minutes, stirring occasionally. Spoon the tuna mixture into a 9×9-inch baking dish and sprinkle with the cheese.

3 Bake in a preheated 325-degree oven for 15 to 20 minutes. If time is of the essence, omit the baking time and serve straight from the saucepan.

Yield: 8 (1-cup) servings

Inside-Out Sandwiches

2 tablespoons cream cheese

2 tablespoons processed
cheese spread

2 teaspoons chopped green onions

1 teaspoon mustard

12 slices various cold cuts
(turkey, ham, salami)

4 large breadsticks

Nutritional Profiles 230–233

1 Combine the cream cheese, cheese spread, green onions and mustard in a bowl and mix well. Arrange three slices of the cold cuts overlapping on a sheet of plastic wrap. Spread one-fourth of the cream cheese mixture evenly on the cold cuts, covering the slices completely.

2 Place one breadstick at the bottom edge of the cold cut slices and roll the slices around the breadstick. Repeat the process with the remaining cold cuts, remaining cream cheese mixture and remaining breadsticks. Chill, covered, until set.

Yield: 4 servings

Tootie's Elvis Sandwich

2 tablespoons smooth or crunchy peanut butter

2 slices whole wheat bread

1 banana, sliced

1 teaspoon honey

1 Spread the peanut butter over one slice of the bread. Layer the banana slices over the peanut butter and drizzle with the honey. Top with the remaining slice of bread. Cut as desired.

Yield: 1 serving

Nutritional Profiles 230–233

Glazed Carrots

1 pound baby carrots

1/4 cup water

1/4 cup maple syrup

3 tablespoons unsalted butter

2 tablespoons orange juice

1/2 teaspoon cinnamon

1/4 teaspoon ground allspice

1/4 teaspoon salt

1 Combine the carrots, water, syrup, butter, orange juice, cinnamon, allspice and salt in a saucepan and mix well. Bring to a boil over high heat.

2 Reduce the heat and cook for 15 minutes or until the carrots are tender and the sauce is of a glaze consistency, stirring occasionally.

Yield: 6 (1/2-cup) servings

Nutritional Profiles 230–233

Natsha's Apple Cheese Casserole

Serve hot or chilled as a side dish or for dessert topped with vanilla ice cream.

1 1/2 cups sugar

1 1/2 cups all-purpose flour

1 cup (2 sticks) margarine

1 pound Velveeta
cheese, shredded

2 (20-ounce) cans sliced
apples, drained

1 (21-ounce) can apple pie filling

1 Combine the sugar, flour, margarine and cheese in a blender and process until smooth and creamy. Mix the apples and apple pie filling in a 9×13-inch baking dish.

2 Spread the creamed mixture over the apple layer. Bake in a preheated 350-degree oven for 30 to 45 minutes or until the top begins to brown.

Yield: 16 (1/2-cup) servings

Nutritional Profiles 230–233

Oven-Baked Cauliflower

1 cup light mayonnaise

1 head cauliflower,
broken into florets

1 cup Italian-style bread crumbs

Nutritional Profiles 230–233

1 Place the mayonnaise in a large heavy-duty sealable plastic bag. Add the cauliflower and seal tightly. Shake to coat.

2 Add the bread crumbs to the bag and seal tightly. Shake to coat.

3 Spread the coated cauliflower in a single layer on a lightly greased baking sheet. Bake in a preheated 350-degree oven for 45 minutes.

Yield: 8 (2-ounce) servings

Zucchini Crispies

3 zucchini

1/4 cup ranch salad dressing

1/2 cup dry seasoned bread crumbs

Nutritional Profiles 230–233

1 Cut the zucchini into 1/4-inch slices. Spread one side of each zucchini slice with some of the salad dressing and immediately dip the dressing side of the slices in the bread crumbs.

2 Arrange the slices crumb side up on a baking sheet. Bake in a preheated 400-degree oven for 20 minutes or until light brown. This is very easy for children to prepare. They will only need help slicing the zucchini and taking the crispies in and out of the oven.

Yield: 6 servings

Biscuits

Substitute skim milk for the buttermilk, if desired.

2 cups all-purpose flour

4 teaspoons baking powder

1 teaspoon salt

$^1/_2$ cup Crisco

$^1/_2$ teaspoon baking soda

1 cup buttermilk or skim milk

2 tablespoons Crisco

Nutritional Profiles 230–233

1 Sift the flour, baking powder and salt together into a bowl. Cut in $^1/_2$ cup shortening until crumbly using a pastry cutter or fork. Dissolve the baking soda in the buttermilk in a bowl and add to the flour mixture. Stir until combined.

2 Knead the dough until a rough ball forms; turn the dough onto a lightly floured surface. Roll to the desired thickness and cut into twelve rounds using a biscuit cutter. Microwave 2 tablespoons shortening in a microwave-safe bowl until melted. Dip the tops and bottoms of each round in the shortening and arrange the rounds on a baking sheet. Bake in a preheated 500-degree oven for 12 minutes or until golden brown.

Yield: 12 biscuits

Be sure to stress the importance of cleanliness where food preparation and consumption is concerned. Keep work areas, utensils, and food ingredients clean and sanitary. Washing hands before and after preparing or eating meals prevents the spreading of germs. **A clean-up tip from a Crescent City Cutie:** *"I like to help by cleaning the table. It is my favorite because it is easy to clean."*
—Elizabeth "Lizzie" Robert

Corn Bread

2 cups yellow cornmeal

1 cup all-purpose flour

3/4 cup sugar

3 tablespoons baking powder

1 1/2 teaspoons salt

1 cup sour cream

1 cup canned cream-style corn

1/2 cup (1 stick)
margarine, melted

2 eggs, beaten

1 cup milk

Nutritional Profiles 230–233

1 Combine the cornmeal, flour, sugar, baking powder and salt in a bowl and mix well. Stir in the sour cream, corn, margarine and eggs. Add the milk and mix well.

2 Spoon the cornmeal mixture into twelve greased muffin cups or spread in a greased 9×13-inch baking pan.

3 Bake in a preheated 400-degree oven for 15 to 30 minutes or until brown. Serve with butter and cane syrup for a real treat.

Yield: 12 muffins

Georgia's Sweet Potato
Apple Muffins

6 tablespoons granulated sugar

1 tablespoon cinnamon

2 cups all-purpose flour

1 teaspoon baking soda

1 teaspoon salt

1 teaspoon ginger powder

1 teaspoon cinnamon

1/2 teaspoon nutmeg

1/2 teaspoon ground cloves

1/2 cup (1 stick) butter, softened

1/2 cup packed dark brown sugar

1/2 cup granulated sugar

2 eggs

1 1/3 cups mashed baked sweet potato (1 large sweet potato)

2 Granny smith apples, peeled and chopped

1/2 cup milk

1/2 teaspoon vanilla extract

1 Mix 6 tablespoons granulated sugar and 1 tablespoon cinnamon in a bowl. Whisk the flour, baking soda, salt, ginger, 1 teaspoon cinnamon, the nutmeg and cloves in a bowl.

2 Beat the butter in a mixing bowl until creamy. Add the brown sugar and 1/2 cup granulated sugar and beat until light and fluffy.

3 Add the eggs one at a time, beating well after each addition. Beat in the sweet potato, apples, milk and vanilla; the batter may appear curdled. Add the flour mixture and beat just until combined.

4 Fill twenty-four greased muffin cups halfway full with the batter and sprinkle evenly with the cinnamon-sugar mixture.

5 Bake in a preheated 350-degree oven for 18 minutes or until a wooden pick inserted in the center comes out clean. Cool in the pan for 2 minutes and remove to a wire rack.

Yield: 24 muffins

Nutritional Profiles 230–233

Whole Grain Waffles

1 1/4 cups all-purpose flour

3/4 cup rolled oats

1/4 cup packed light brown sugar

2 tablespoons wheat germ

4 teaspoons baking powder

1 teaspoon cinnamon

1/2 teaspoon fine salt

2 eggs

1 1/2 cups milk

1/4 cup (1/2 stick) unsalted butter, melted

1/4 cup peanut oil or walnut oil

Nutritional Profiles 230–233

1 Whisk the flour, oats, brown sugar, wheat germ, baking powder, cinnamon and salt in a bowl.

2 Whisk the eggs in a bowl until blended. Add the milk, butter and peanut oil and mix well.

3 Add the egg mixture to the dry ingredients and stir with a wooden spoon just until combined, leaving a few lumps.

4 Heat a waffle iron to medium-high. Pour 1/3 to 1/2 cup of the batter per waffle onto the hot waffle iron. Cook for 3 to 5 minutes or until the waffles are crisp. Serve with warm maple syrup.

Yield: 4 servings

Pumpkin Dip

Serve as a dessert or as a dip.

1 (7-ounce) jar
marshmallow creme

8 ounces cream cheese, softened

1 (21-ounce) can pumpkin
pie filling

1 Combine the marshmallow creme, cream cheese and pie filling in a bowl and stir until combined.

2 Serve with graham crackers or Teddy Grahams.

Yield: 20 (2-ounce) servings

Nutritional Profiles 230–233

Chocolate Popcorn Clusters

12 cups popped
unseasoned popcorn

3 cups salted peanuts or cashews

1³/4 cups semisweet
chocolate chips

1 cup corn syrup

1/4 cup (1/2 stick) butter

1 Toss the popcorn and peanuts in a greased large roasting pan. Combine the chocolate chips, corn syrup and butter in a small saucepan.

2 Cook over low heat until the mixture is smooth and just comes to a boil, stirring occasionally. Remove from the heat and pour over the popcorn mixture. Toss to coat.

3 Bake in a preheated 300-degree oven for 35 to 40 minutes, stirring every 10 minutes. Spread the popcorn mixture on a baking sheet lined with waxed paper. Let stand until cool.

Nutritional Profiles 230–233

4 Break evenly into twenty-four clusters. Store in an airtight container.

Yield: 24 clusters

S'mores Pops

2 cups graham cracker crumbs

1 (16-ounce) package
chocolate chips

1 (16-ounce) package
large marshmallows

Nutritional Profiles 230–233

1 Place the graham cracker crumbs in a shallow dish. Heat the chocolate chips in a double boiler over simmering water until smooth, stirring occasionally.

2 Spear each marshmallow with a wooden pick. Dip the marshmallows in the chocolate until coated and then coat with the cracker crumbs. Place the pops on a sheet of waxed paper and let stand until set.

Yield: 20 pops

Zebras

1 (8-ounce) package vanilla
instant pudding mix

1 (8-ounce) package chocolate
instant pudding mix

8 maraschino cherries

Nutritional Profiles 230–233

1 Prepare the vanilla pudding and chocolate pudding separately using the package directions and substituting low-fat milk for the whole milk.

2 Layer the vanilla pudding and chocolate pudding alternately in 1-inch layers in parfait glasses. Top each parfait with 1 maraschino cherry. Chill until serving time.

Yield: 8 servings

Photograph for this recipe on page 54.

Frozen Banana Pops

4 bananas

1 (16-ounce) package milk chocolate chips

1 1/2 cups granola cereal without raisins

Nutritional Profiles 230–233

1 Cut the bananas into halves and insert a popsicle stick in the cut end of each banana half. Arrange in a single layer on a baking sheet lined with waxed paper. Freeze for 1 hour.

2 Melt the chocolate chips in a saucepan over low heat, stirring frequently. Dip the frozen bananas in the chocolate and then roll in the cereal. Arrange the pops on the same baking sheet and freeze for 8 to 10 hours. Let stand at room temperature for 10 minutes before serving.

Yield: 8 pops

Madeline's Fresh Lemon Ice Cream

1 (12-ounce) can fat-free evaporated milk

3/4 cup sugar

1/2 cup fresh lemon juice

Nutritional Profiles 230–233

1 Pour the evaporated milk into a 1 1/2-quart freezer-safe mixing bowl. Freeze until of a slushy consistency. Beat at high speed until soft peaks form. Add the sugar, beating constantly until blended. Add the lemon juice and beat until the consistency of whipped cream.

2 Freeze, covered, until firm. Spoon the ice cream into dessert bowls and serve with fresh strawberries, fresh blueberries and/or fresh sliced peaches.

Yield: 8 servings

Blueberry Oatmeal Bars

2 cups old-fashioned oats

1 1/4 cups all-purpose flour

1/2 cup sugar

1 teaspoon vanilla extract

1/2 teaspoon cinnamon

1/4 teaspoon baking powder

1/4 teaspoon salt (optional)

3/4 cup Smart Balance trans fat-free buttery spread, chilled

1 cup low-sugar blueberry preserves

1/2 cup spinach purée

Nutritional Profiles 230–233

1 Whisk the oats, flour, sugar, vanilla, cinnamon, baking powder and salt in a bowl. Add the buttery spread and mix with two knives until the mixture resembles coarse meal. Pieces of the butter should be visible. Do not overmix.

2 Reserve half the oats mixture. Press the remaining oats mixture over the bottom of an 8×8-inch baking pan sprayed with nonstick cooking spray.

3 Bake in a preheated 375-degree oven for 13 to 15 minutes or until the edges are light brown. The layer will not be fully baked. Maintain the oven temperature.

4 Mix the preserves and spinach purée in a bowl. Spread over the baked layer and sprinkle with the reserved oats mixture.

5 Bake for 20 to 25 minutes or until light brown. Cool in the pan on a wire rack. Cut into twelve bars.

Yield: 12 bars

Yogurt Pie

3 (6-ounce) containers any flavor yogurt

8 ounces whipped topping

I baked (9-inch) pie shell

Chopped or sliced fresh fruit to match yogurt flavor (optional)

Nutritional Profiles 230–233

1 Combine the yogurt and whipped topping in a bowl and mix well. Spread in the pie shell.

2 Freeze until firm. Thaw slightly and top with the fruit before serving.

Yield: 8 servings

Sometimes adding a favorite ingredient to any recipe will help make it appealing to even the pickiest eater. Simply top your dish with whatever a doubtful child likes to eat most. Sprinkle cheese on vegetables, slice fruit into oatmeal, throw raisins into rice, or toss nuts into soup. There are no rules! **A garnish tip from a Crescent City Cutie:** *"I'll eat anything with fruit or yogurt on top."*

—Cali Jane Luetkemeier

Crescent City Cool Kids

Teenage years can be a challenging time for parents as children are growing to become young adults. Parents continue to guide their children in making good decisions, some of which will inevitably involve food choices. With busy schedules, teens notoriously do not want to take time for well-balanced meals and often resort to fast-food options. Keeping quick and easy-to-prepare foods and recipes available can be valuable tools for these busy years, and a little advance planning can go a long way.

Daily energy requirements for teens ages fourteen to eighteen are approximately 1,800 calories for females and 2,200 calories for males. Daily nutrient requirements include five to six ounces of meat, six to seven ounces of grains, two cups of fruit, two to three cups of vegetables, and three cups of milk.

This is a good age to remind kids that a healthy diet is critical for the final stages of growth and development.

Berry Banana Smoothie

1 ripe banana, chopped

1 cup frozen berries (blueberries, strawberries and raspberries)

3/4 cup orange juice

1/2 cup lemon yogurt

2 ounces soft tofu

2 tablespoons honey

1 Combine the banana, berries, orange juice, yogurt, tofu and honey in a blender. Process until smooth.

2 Pour equal portions of the smoothie into two glasses and serve immediately.

Yield: 2 servings

Photograph for this recipe on page 92.

Nutritional Profiles 230–233

Garden Dip

8 ounces whipped cream cheese

1/3 cup low-fat sour cream

2 tablespoons lemon juice

1/2 envelope Italian salad dressing mix (such as Good Seasons)

1/2 cup chopped celery

1/2 cup chopped red onion

1 Combine the cream cheese, sour cream, lemon juice and salad dressing mix in a bowl and mix well.

2 Stir in the celery and onion. Serve chilled with pita crisps and/or carrot sticks.

Yield: 10 (2-tablespoon) servings

Nutritional Profiles 230–233

Fruit Salsa
and Cinnamon Chips

Cinnamon Chips

1/2 cup sugar

1/4 cup cinnamon

4 (6-inch) flour tortillas

Fruit Salsa

2 kiwifruit, chopped

2 Golden Delicious apples, peeled and chopped

2 McIntosh apples, peeled and chopped

1 pound strawberries, sliced or chopped

8 ounces raspberries

8 ounces blueberries

1/4 cup orange juice

3 tablespoons fig preserves

1 tablespoon brown sugar

1 For the chips, mix the sugar and cinnamon in a bowl. Cut each tortilla into eight triangles. Spray both sides of the triangles with olive oil nonstick cooking spray and sprinkle both sides with the cinnamon-sugar mixture.

2 Arrange the triangles in a single layer on a baking sheet. Bake in a preheated 350-degree oven for 8 to 10 minutes or until light brown. Remove to a wire rack to cool.

3 For the salsa, toss the kiwifruit, apples, strawberries, raspberries and blueberries in a bowl.

4 Mix the orange juice, fig preserves and brown sugar in a bowl and add to the fruit mixture, stirring until coated. Chill, covered, for 30 minutes. Serve with the chips.

Yield: 6 servings

Nutritional Profiles 230–233

Jen's Vegetable Square
Appetizers

2 (8-count) cans crescent rolls

16 ounces cream cheese, softened

1 envelope Hidden Valley ranch salad dressing mix

1 cup (4 ounces) shredded Cheddar cheese

1 cup chopped broccoli

1 cup chopped cauliflower

1 cup chopped black olives

1 cup chopped seeded tomatoes

1/2 cup chopped green onions

Nutritional Profiles 230–233

1 Unroll the crescent roll dough and spread on a baking sheet, pressing the edges and perforations to seal.

2 Bake in a preheated 375-degree oven for 13 to 15 minutes or until light brown. Let stand until cool.

3 Mix the cream cheese and dressing mix in a bowl. Spread the cream cheese mixture over the baked layer.

4 Gently toss the Cheddar cheese, broccoli, cauliflower, olives, tomatoes and green onions in a bowl.

5 Sprinkle the vegetable mixture evenly over the cream cheese layer. Cut into 1- to 2-inch squares.

Yield: 12 servings

Photograph for this recipe on page 92.

As teens grow, their schedules become busier. A meal is often "on the go," but this does not mean one must sacrifice nutritional content. Keep a supply of healthful snacks available. **A snack tip from a Crescent City Cool Kid:** *"My favorite foods are leftovers, something you can eat at any time of the day."*

—Daniel Hernandez

Tricolor Pasta Salad

14 ounces tricolor tortellini

1 pound fresh or frozen chopped cauliflower, carrots and broccoli

12 ounces fresh or frozen green peas

2 (2-ounce) cans sliced black olives, drained

3/4 cup (3 ounces) grated Parmesan cheese

1/4 cup mayonnaise

1 tablespoon coarsely ground pepper

1 teaspoon salt

Nutritional Profiles 230–233

1 Cook the pasta in boiling water in a saucepan for 10 minutes; drain. Steam the cauliflower mixture and peas in a steamer; drain.

2 Combine the pasta, vegetables and olives in a bowl and mix gently.

3 Add the cheese, mayonnaise, pepper and salt to the pasta mixture and toss to combine. Serve warm or chilled.

Yield: 8 servings

Cowboy Salad

I pound extra-lean ground beef
(at least 93% fat-free)

Tony Chachere's Creole seasoning
to taste

I (15-ounce) can ranch-style
pinto beans

2 ripe tomatoes, sliced

2 green onions, sliced

I cup (4 ounces) shredded
Cheddar cheese

1/4 cup Catalina Salad Dressing
(page 79)

Nutritional Profiles 230–233

1 Season the ground beef with the Cajun seasoning. Brown the ground beef in a skillet, stirring until crumbly; drain.

2 Combine the ground beef, beans, tomatoes, green onions, cheese and dressing in a salad bowl and mix well.

Yield: 4 servings

Catalina Salad Dressing

1 cup sugar

1 cup olive oil

2/3 cup ketchup

1/2 cup vinegar

2 teaspoons sea salt

1/2 teaspoon chili powder

1/2 teaspoon celery seeds

1/2 teaspoon dry mustard

Dash of paprika

1 Combine the sugar, olive oil, ketchup, vinegar, salt, chili powder, celery seeds, dry mustard and paprika in a blender and process until combined.

2 Pour the dressing into a jar with a tight-fitting lid and seal tightly. Store in the refrigerator. Shake before serving.

Yield: 8 (2-ounce) servings

Nutritional Profiles 230–233

Roasted Pecan Balsamic Dressing

Drizzle the dressing over grilled chicken breasts on lettuce-lined salad plates. It's also good over salads containing fresh fruit such as grapes, mandarin oranges, and/or mangoes.

1/2 cup pecans

1 cup olive oil

1/2 cup balsamic vinegar

1/2 cup crumbled feta cheese or blue cheese

1/3 cup packed brown sugar

1 tablespoon dry mustard

1/2 teaspoon pepper

1/4 teaspoon salt

1 Break the pecans into pieces and spread on a baking sheet. Toast in a preheated 350-degree oven for 10 minutes. Remove to a plate to cool.

2 Combine the pecans, olive oil, vinegar, cheese, brown sugar, dry mustard, pepper and salt in a jar with a tight-fitting lid and seal tightly. Shake to combine. Chill for 1 hour or longer. Shake before serving.

Yield: 24 (1-ounce) servings

Nutritional Profiles 230–233

Crispy Noodle Coleslaw

Coleslaw Dressing

1 (3-ounce) package chicken-flavored ramen noodles with seasoning packet

2/3 cup vegetable oil

3 tablespoons red wine vinegar

1/4 cup sugar or Splenda

Coleslaw

4 cups angel hair coleslaw

1/2 cup sliced almonds, toasted

3 ounces sunflower seeds

3 green onions, chopped

Nutritional Profiles 230–233

1 For the dressing, reserve the noodles for the salad. Combine the seasoning packet, oil, vinegar and sugar in a pint jar with a tight-fitting lid and seal tightly. Shake to mix. Chill for 8 to 10 hours.

2 For the coleslaw, break the reserved noodles into pieces and place in a bowl. Add the coleslaw, almonds, sunflower seeds and green onions and toss to combine. Add the dressing just before serving and mix well.

Yield: 12 servings

Noah's Tender
Slow-Cooker Brisket

1 (10-pound) brisket

Creole seasoning to taste

2 cups ketchup

1 cup packed brown sugar

1 (10-ounce) can tomato soup

2 tablespoons liquid smoke

2 tablespoons spicy mustard

2 tablespoons
Worcestershire sauce

3/4 cup sour cream

1 teaspoon prepared horseradish

Nutritional Profiles 230–233

1 Trim any excess fat from the brisket and season liberally with Creole seasoning. Place in a slow cooker.

2 Combine the ketchup, brown sugar, soup, liquid smoke, mustard and Worcestershire sauce in a bowl and mix well. Pour over the brisket.

3 Cook on Low for 4 to 6 hours or until the brisket is very tender. Remove the brisket to a platter, reserving the pan drippings. Skim any fat from the drippings.

4 Combine 1 cup of the reserved drippings, the sour cream and horseradish in a bowl and mix well. Serve with the brisket.

Yield: 10 servings

Italian Beef

1 (5-pound) beef rump roast

2 garlic cloves, cut into slivers

1 tablespoon fennel seeds

6 beef bouillon cubes

3 cups boiling water

1/2 cup chopped green bell pepper

1 garlic clove, minced

2 tablespoons Worcestershire sauce

1 teaspoon marjoram

1 teaspoon oregano

1 teaspoon thyme

1 teaspoon salt

1 teaspoon pepper

1 teaspoon Tabasco sauce

1 green bell pepper, cut into 10 slices

2 tablespoons olive oil

Nutritional Profiles 230–233

1 Make slashes in the roast on all sides and insert the garlic slivers into the slashes. Place the roast in a Dutch oven and sprinkle with the fennel seeds. Dissolve the bouillon cubes in the boiling water in a heatproof bowl and pour around the roast.

2 Roast in a preheated 325-degree oven for 1 hour and 40 minutes. Remove the roast to a platter, reserving the pan drippings. Chill the roast in the refrigerator; slice as desired.

3 Stir 1/2 cup chopped bell pepper, 1 garlic clove, the Worcestershire sauce, marjoram, oregano, thyme, salt, pepper and Tabasco sauce into the reserved pan drippings. Simmer over low heat for 15 minutes, stirring occasionally.

4 Pour the gravy over the sliced roast. Marinate, covered, in the refrigerator for 4 to 10 hours.

5 Reheat the roast and gravy. Sauté the bell pepper slices in the olive oil in a skillet until tender. Serve the sliced roast topped with the sautéed bell pepper. For variety, serve over slices of Italian bread.

Yield: 10 servings

Awesome Spaghetti

10 ounces vermicelli

2 pounds ground round

3 (8-ounce) cans tomato sauce

1 large onion, chopped

1/2 large green bell pepper, chopped

1/4 cup chopped parsley

1 teaspoon Italian herbs

8 ounces fat-free cream cheese

2 cups fat-free cottage cheese

1/2 cup fat-free sour cream

1/2 cup (2 ounces) shredded Cheddar cheese

Nutritional Profiles 230–233

1 Cook the pasta using the package directions; drain. Brown the ground round in a skillet, stirring until crumbly; drain.

2 Stir in the tomato sauce, onion, bell pepper, parsley and herbs. Cook until the onion is tender, stirring occasionally.

3 Beat the cream cheese, cottage cheese and sour cream in a mixing bowl until smooth. Layer the pasta, cream cheese mixture, ground round mixture and Cheddar cheese in the order listed in a 2-quart baking dish.

4 Bake in a preheated 350-degree oven for 30 to 40 minutes or until heated through. You may prepare in advance and freeze for future use.

Yield: 10 servings

Pork Chops and Apples

1 cup all-purpose flour

2 tablespoons salt

6 (6-ounce) thick-cut pork chops

$^1/_4$ cup vegetable oil

6 tablespoons butter

2 green apples, sliced

$^3/_4$ cup packed brown sugar

$^1/_4$ teaspoon cinnamon

Nutritional Profiles 230–233

1 Mix the flour and salt in a shallow dish or in a sealable plastic bag. Coat the pork chops with the flour mixture.

2 Fry the pork chops in the oil in a skillet until cooked through and brown on both sides; drain. Arrange the pork chops in a single layer in a 9×13-inch baking dish.

3 Melt the butter in a skillet and add the apples. Sauté the apples in the butter. Sprinkle with the brown sugar and cinnamon and sauté until the brown sugar melts.

4 Spoon the apple mixture over the pork chops. Bake, covered with foil, in a preheated 300-degree oven for 20 minutes.

Yield: 6 servings

Spaghetti alla Carbonara

16 ounces spaghetti

4 ounces thick-sliced smoked bacon or prosciutto, chopped

3 tablespoons olive oil

1/3 cup chopped onion

5 eggs

1/4 cup (1 ounce) grated Parmesan cheese

Salt and pepper to taste

1 tablespoon butter

Nutritional Profiles 230–233

1 Cook the pasta in boiling water in a saucepan until tender. Sauté the bacon in the olive oil in a skillet; add the onion. Sauté until the onion is tender.

2 Beat the eggs in a bowl until blended. Stir in the cheese, salt and pepper.

3 Drain the pasta and return to the saucepan. Immediately mix in the hot bacon mixture and butter. Stir in the egg mixture. The hot bacon mixture should cook the eggs as you stir. If it does not, cook over low heat for a few seconds longer.

Yield: 4 servings

Chicken Piccata

1/2 cup all-purpose flour

1/2 teaspoon black pepper

1/2 teaspoon paprika

1/2 teaspoon cayenne pepper

4 (4-ounce) boneless
skinless chicken breasts

2 tablespoons unsalted butter

1 tablespoon olive oil

1/2 cup lemon juice

1/4 cup madeira

1/4 cup capers

Nutritional Profiles 230–233

1　Mix the flour, black pepper, paprika and cayenne pepper in a shallow dish. Coat the chicken in the flour mixture.

2　Heat the butter and olive oil in a skillet until the butter melts. Sauté the chicken in the butter mixture until the chicken is cooked through. Remove the chicken to a platter using a slotted spoon, reserving the pan drippings. Cover to keep warm.

3　Stir the lemon juice, wine and capers into the reserved pan drippings and bring to a boil. Pour over the chicken.

Yield: 4 servings

Creamy Chicken Lasagna

4 (4-ounce) chicken breasts, boiled or poached

9 lasagna noodles

1 tablespoon butter or margarine

8 ounces mushrooms, sliced

1/3 cup butter

1/3 cup all-purpose flour

3 cups milk

1 1/2 cups (6 ounces) freshly grated Parmesan cheese

1/2 cup whipping cream

3/4 teaspoon dried basil

1/2 teaspoon salt

1/4 teaspoon freshly ground pepper

2 cups (8 ounces) shredded mozzarella cheese

Nutritional Profiles 230–233

1 Chop the chicken into bite-size pieces and place in a bowl. Cook the pasta using the package directions; drain. Arrange the pasta in a single layer on a sheet of waxed paper.

2 Heat 1 tablespoon butter in a large skillet over medium-high heat until melted. Add the mushrooms and cook until the mushrooms are tender, stirring constantly; drain. Mix the mushrooms with the chicken. Heat 1/3 cup butter in a skillet until melted and stir in the flour. Cook for 1 minute, stirring constantly. Add the milk gradually, stirring constantly.

3 Cook for about 3 minutes or until bubbly, stirring constantly. Stir in the Parmesan cheese, cream, basil, salt and pepper. Cook until the cheese melts and the sauce is thickened, stirring frequently. Stir the chicken mixture into the cheese sauce.

4 Layer the chicken mixture and pasta one-third at a time in a 2-quart baking dish coated with nonstick cooking spray, ending with the pasta. Sprinkle with the mozzarella cheese. Garnish with paprika and chopped fresh parsley. Bake in a preheated 350-degree oven for 30 minutes.

Yield: 10 servings

Feta-Stuffed Chicken

1/4 cup basil-tomato feta cheese

2 tablespoons tub-style light cream cheese

1 tablespoon chopped fresh mint

4 (5-ounce) boneless skinless chicken breasts

1/2 teaspoon kosher salt

1/4 teaspoon freshly ground pepper

1 tablespoon extra-virgin olive oil

1/4 cup chicken broth

10 ounces fresh spinach

2 tablespoons walnut or pecan pieces

1 tablespoon lemon juice

Nutritional Profiles 230–233

1 Mix the feta cheese, cream cheese and mint in a bowl. Cut a 1 1/2-inch horizontal slit 1 inch deep through the thickest portion of each chicken breast to form a pocket. Stuff the pockets evenly with the cheese mixture. Secure with wooden picks. Sprinkle with the salt and pepper.

2 Heat the olive oil in a large nonstick skillet over medium-high heat. Add the stuffed chicken breasts and cook for 12 to 15 minutes or until a meat thermometer registers 170 degrees and the chicken is no longer pink internally, turning occasionally to brown evenly. Reduce the heat to medium if the chicken browns too quickly. Remove the chicken to a platter and cover to keep warm, reserving the pan drippings.

3 Cool the pan drippings for 1 minute. Add the broth to the reserved pan drippings gradually and bring to a boil. Add the spinach gradually and cook for 2 to 3 minutes or until the spinach wilts, turning with tongs. Stir in the walnuts and lemon juice.

4 Divide the spinach mixture evenly among four serving plates and top each serving with one chicken breast. Garnish with lemon slices. You may substitute a mixture of 1 teaspoon snipped drained oil-pack sun-dried tomatoes and 1/4 cup crumbled feta cheese for the basil-tomato feta cheese.

Yield: 4 servings

Photograph for this recipe appears on page 92.

Homemade Chicken Potpie

2 potatoes, peeled and cut into bite-size pieces

2 carrots, peeled and cut into bite-size pieces

1 cup frozen peas

1 cup frozen corn

3 tablespoons olive oil

2 (4-ounce) boneless skinless chicken breasts, cut into bite-size pieces

1 tablespoon Italian seasoning

Salt and pepper to taste

1 envelope chicken gravy mix, prepared

2 unbaked (9-inch) pie shells (do not thaw)

1 Combine the potatoes and carrots with enough water to cover in a large saucepan. Add the peas and corn and bring to a boil. Boil until the potatoes are tender; drain.

2 Heat the olive oil in a skillet; add the chicken, Italian seasoning, salt and pepper. Cook until the chicken is cooked through, stirring frequently. Stir in the potato mixture and gravy.

3 Spoon the chicken mixture into one of the pie shells. Top with the remaining pie shell, sealing the edge and cutting vents. Bake using the pie shell directions.

Yield: 6 servings

Nutritional Profiles 230–233

Pita Pocket Sandwich

I whole wheat pita pocket, toasted

2 ounces sliced roasted turkey

I ounce Pepper Jack cheese

I tablespoon guacamole

2 slices tomato

1/2 cup shredded lettuce, bean sprouts or alfalfa sprouts

1 Stuff the pita pocket with the turkey, cheese, guacamole, tomato and lettuce. Serve immediately.

Yield: I serving

Photograph for this recipe on page 92.

Nutritional Profiles 230–233

Baked Catfish

6 (6-ounce) catfish fillets

1/4 teaspoon salt

1/4 teaspoon black pepper

1 1/2 cups panko

1/4 teaspoon salt

1/4 teaspoon garlic powder

1/8 teaspoon ground red pepper

4 egg whites

1 Sprinkle the fillets with 1/4 teaspoon salt and the black pepper. Mix the bread crumbs, 1/4 teaspoon salt, the garlic powder and red pepper in a shallow dish. Whisk the egg whites in a bowl until frothy. Dip the fillets in the egg whites and coat with the bread crumb mixture. Lightly coat both sides of the fillets with nonstick cooking spray. Arrange the fillets in a single layer on a wire rack coated with nonstick cooking spray. Place the rack on a 10×15-inch baking sheet lined with foil.

2 Bake in a preheated 375-degree oven for 25 to 30 minutes or until the fillets are golden brown and flake easily. Garnish with sprigs of parsley and lemon slices.

Yield: 6 servings

Nutritional Profiles 230–233

Crawfish Pasta

The pasta dish has several ingredients, but most of them are common to any pantry. It is such an easy dish to prepare and always a crowd pleaser.

1/2 cup (1 stick) butter

1 small onion, chopped

4 green onions, chopped

2 ribs celery, chopped

1 pound crawfish

1 garlic clove, chopped

1 tablespoon all-purpose flour

1 1/2 cups half-and-half

1 tablespoon parsley flakes

1/2 teaspoon salt

1/4 teaspoon pepper

2 capfuls liquid crab boil, or to taste

16 ounces pasta, cooked and drained

1/2 cup (2 ounces) grated Parmesan cheese

1 Melt the butter in a large skillet and add the onion, green onions and celery. Cook until the vegetables are tender. Stir in the crawfish and garlic and simmer for 5 minutes.

2 Whisk in the flour and cook for 2 minutes. Add the half-and-half, parsley flakes, salt, pepper and crab boil and mix well. Simmer just until heated through, stirring occasionally.

3 Pour the crawfish mixture over the pasta in a serving bowl and sprinkle with the cheese. Garnish with parsley. Serve immediately with a green salad and crusty French bread. You may substitute shrimp for the crawfish.

Yield: 6 servings

Photograph for this recipe on page 92.

Nutritional Profiles 230–233

Crawfish Pie

1 pound crawfish tails

1/4 cup (1/2 stick) butter

1/2 cup chopped fresh parsley, or
1 tablespoon parsley flakes

1 onion, chopped

3 green onions, chopped

1/2 cup (1 stick) butter

3 tablespoons all-purpose flour

2 cups half-and-half

3 tablespoons sherry

Salt and black pepper to taste

Cayenne pepper to taste

2 unbaked (9-inch) deep-dish
pie shells

Nutritional Profiles 230–233

1 Sauté the crawfish tails in 1/4 cup butter in a skillet for 10 minutes. Sauté the parsley, onion and green onions in 1/2 cup butter in a skillet until the onions are tender. Blend in the flour and cook until bubbly, stirring constantly.

2 Stir in the half-and-half and cook until thickened. Mix in the sherry and crawfish tails. Season with salt, black pepper and cayenne pepper.

3 Spoon the crawfish mixture into one of the pie shells. Top with the remaining pie shell, sealing the edge and cutting vents.

4 Bake in a preheated 350-degree oven for 20 minutes. Freeze for future use, if desired.

Yield: 8 servings

Shrimp Appaloosa

I pound shrimp, peeled and deveined

1 1/2 cups rice, rinsed

I cup beef broth

I (4-ounce) can sliced mushrooms

1/2 cup (1 stick) margarine, melted

I onion, chopped

I bunch green onion bulbs and some tops, chopped

Nutritional Profiles 230–233

1 Combine the shrimp, rice, broth, mushrooms, margarine, onion and green onions in a rice cooker and stir.

2 Cook over low to medium heat using the rice cooker directions for about 20 to 30 minutes or until the rice is tender and the shrimp are pink.

Yield: 6 servings

The quality and freshness of each ingredient that goes into a recipe is important. Everything used in a dish determines how delicious and healthful it will be. So too is every component of an entire meal important. Keep each meal balanced and include foods from every important group. **A balanced meal idea from a Crescent City Cutie:** *"spaghetti with sauce, strawberries, and bubble water to drink."*
—Marguerite Schwarz

Jambalaya

2 pounds cooked deveined
peeled shrimp

2 pounds chicken, cooked
and chopped

2 pounds sausage, sliced

1/4 cup vegetable oil

I onion, chopped

I bunch green onions, chopped

I bell pepper, chopped

I rib celery with leaves, chopped

8 garlic cloves, chopped

2 cups uncooked rice

I tomato, chopped

I (16-ounce) can stewed
tomatoes, drained

3 cups seafood stock

I seafood bouillon cube

I chicken bouillon cube

5 bay leaves

2 teaspoons Creole seasoning

Tabasco sauce to taste

1 Sauté the shrimp, chicken and sausage in the oil in a stockpot. Add half the onion, half the green onions, half the bell pepper, half the celery and half the garlic and mix well.

2 Sauté for 10 minutes. Mix in the remaining onion, remaining green onions, remaining bell pepper, remaining celery, remaining garlic, the rice and tomato.

3 Stir in the stock, bouillon cubes, bay leaves, Creole seasoning and Tabasco sauce. Bring to a boil and boil for 5 minutes or until most of the liquid is absorbed. Reduce the heat.

4 Simmer, covered, for 30 minutes. Remove from the heat and let stand for 10 minutes. Discard the bay leaves.

Yield: 12 servings

Nutritional Profiles 230–233

Cheesy Eggplant "Lasagna"

2¹/2 to 3 pounds eggplant, thinly sliced

1 cup thinly sliced onion

1 cup mushrooms, sliced

1 (14-ounce) can diced tomatoes

1 cup (4 ounces) grated Parmesan cheese

1¹/2 cups (6 ounces) shredded mozzarella cheese

1 (25-ounce) jar Prego tomato sauce

1 teaspoon salt

1 teaspoon pepper

1 teaspoon dried basil

Nutritional Profiles 230–233

1 Layer one-third of the eggplant slices overlapping in a greased 9×13-inch baking dish. Top with half the onion, half the mushrooms, half the tomatoes, ¹/2 cup of the Parmesan cheese and ¹/2 cup of the mozzarella cheese.

2 Layer with half the remaining eggplant, the remaining onion, the remaining mushrooms, the remaining tomatoes, the remaining Parmesan cheese and ¹/2 cup of the remaining mozzarella cheese.

3 Top with the remaining eggplant and the tomato sauce. Sprinkle with the remaining ¹/2 cup mozzarella cheese. Sprinkle with the salt, pepper and basil.

4 Bake, covered, in a preheated 400-degree oven for 45 minutes. Remove the cover and bake for 15 minutes longer or until the top is golden brown and bubbly.

Yield: 8 servings

Daniel's Penne

16 ounces penne

1 onion, chopped

1 tablespoon chopped parsley

2 garlic cloves, minced

1/2 teaspoon oregano

1/2 teaspoon rosemary

1/2 teaspoon sage

1/2 cup olive oil

1 (8-ounce) can tomatoes, puréed

1 cup heavy cream,
at room temperature

1 cup (4 ounces) grated
Parmesan cheese

Nutritional Profiles 230–233

1 Cook the pasta using the package directions until al dente; drain. Cover to keep warm.

2 Sauté the onion, parsley, garlic, oregano, rosemary and sage in the olive oil in a saucepan. Add the tomatoes and mix well.

3 Cook for 15 minutes, stirring occasionally. Stir in the cream and simmer for 5 minutes. Add the cheese and mix well.

4 Combine the sauce and pasta in a bowl and stir until coated. Garnish with additional parsley.

Yield: 4 servings

Spaghetti Casserole

16 ounces spaghetti

1 cup (4 ounces) grated Parmesan cheese

1/2 cup parsley flakes

3 eggs

Salt and pepper to taste

16 ounces mozzarella cheese, shredded

1 (24-ounce) jar spaghetti sauce

Nutritional Profiles 230–233

1 Cook the pasta using the package directions. Drain and rinse with cool water. Place the pasta in a bowl and add the Parmesan cheese and parsley flakes gradually, mixing constantly until combined.

2 Whisk the eggs in a bowl until combined and stir into the pasta mixture. Season with salt and pepper.

3 Alternate layers of the pasta mixture and the mozzarella cheese in a 9×13-inch baking dish sprayed with nonstick cooking spray until all of the ingredients are used.

4 Bake in a preheated 350-degree oven for 25 to 30 minutes or until heated through. Cut into squares and drizzle with the spaghetti sauce.

Yield: 8 servings

Mom's Marinara Sauce

This is a very versatile sauce. Add browned chicken, Italian sausage, or ground beef for a meat sauce. Or add mushrooms and sliced zucchini for a vegetarian version.

1 onion, chopped

2 carrots, peeled and cut into half circles

3 tablespoons olive oil

2 garlic cloves, minced

1 (28-ounce) can crushed tomatoes

1 (8-ounce) can tomato paste

1 to 2 cups water

2 tablespoons Italian seasoning

Salt and black pepper to taste

Crushed red pepper flakes (optional)

Nutritional Profiles 230–233

1 Sauté the onion and carrots in the olive oil in a saucepan for 5 to 7 minutes or until the vegetables are tender. Stir in the garlic and cook for 1 minute.

2 Add the tomatoes, tomato paste, water, Italian seasoning, salt, black pepper and red pepper flakes and mix well. Bring to a boil.

3 Reduce the heat and simmer for about 45 minutes, stirring occasionally and adding water as needed for the desired consistency. You may substitute a mixture of 2 teaspoons dried oregano, 1 teaspoon dried thyme and 1/2 teaspoon rosemary, crushed, for the Italian seasoning. Cut the amounts in half if using fresh herbs. Double or triple the recipe and freeze for future use.

Yield: 8 servings

Healthy Spaghetti Sauce

While it is often easier to use commercially prepared spaghetti sauce, this recipe is healthier because it cuts down on sugar and sodium often found in store-bought sauces. Add steamed vegetables for added nutrition.

1 onion, chopped

1 tablespoon butter, margarine or olive oil

1 bell pepper, chopped

Chopped garlic to taste

Oregano to taste

Italian seasoning to taste

1 carrot, chopped

1 pound ground beef

1 (8-ounce) can Contadina tomato sauce

1 (8-ounce) can Contadina tomato paste

1 Sauté the onion in the butter in a large saucepan. Add the bell pepper and sauté. Stir in the garlic and sauté. Season with oregano and Italian seasoning.

2 Microwave the carrot in a microwave-safe dish for 1 to 2 minutes; stir into the bell pepper mixture.

3 Brown the ground beef in a skillet, stirring until crumbly; drain. Add to the bell pepper mixture and mix well. Stir in the tomato sauce and tomato paste.

4 Simmer over low heat for about 1 hour or to the desired consistency, stirring occasionally. Serve with your favorite pasta, a green salad and garlic bread.

Yield: 6 (1/2-cup) servings

Nutritional Profiles 230–233

Creole Scrambled Eggs

5 eggs

I cup cooked rice

1/2 cup (2 ounces) shredded
Cheddar cheese

1/4 cup chopped green onions

I teaspoon Creole seasoning

I teaspoon Creole mustard

3 tablespoons vegetable oil

Nutritional Profiles 230–233

1 Whisk the eggs in a bowl until blended. Stir in the rice, cheese, green onions, Creole seasoning and Creole mustard.

2 Heat the oil in a skillet and add the egg mixture. Scramble the egg mixture in the hot oil until the desired degree of doneness. Serve immediately.

Yield: 4 servings

Baked Peach French Toast

3 ounces cream cheese, softened

12 (1-inch-thick) slices
French bread

2 (9-ounce) cans sliced
peaches, drained

1/4 cup chopped pecans

1 cup milk

3 eggs

1/3 cup maple syrup

2 tablespoons butter, melted

1 tablespoon sugar

1 teaspoon cinnamon

1 teaspoon vanilla extract

Nutritional Profiles 230–233

1 Spread the cream cheese on both sides of the bread slices and arrange in a 9×13-inch baking pan, overlapping into layers.

2 Prick the bread slices several times with a fork. Top with the peaches and sprinkle with the nuts.

3 Whisk the milk, eggs, syrup, butter, sugar, cinnamon and vanilla in a bowl until combined. Pour over the prepared layers.

4 Bake in a preheated 400-degree oven for 20 to 25 minutes or until set. Serve immediately.

Yield: 8 servings

Puffy Potatoes

6 potatoes, peeled and
cut into chunks

1/4 cup chopped onion

3 tablespoons margarine

1/2 cup (2 ounces) grated
Parmesan cheese

1/4 cup cracker crumbs

1 teaspoon baking powder

Salt and pepper to taste

2 eggs, beaten

Nutritional Profiles 230–233

1 Cook the potatoes in boiling water in a saucepan for 25 minutes or until tender; drain. Mash the potatoes until smooth.

2 Cook the onion in the margarine in a skillet until tender. Stir the onion mixture, cheese, cracker crumbs, baking powder, salt and pepper into the potatoes. Add the eggs and beat until combined.

3 Drop ten mounds of the potato mixture onto a greased baking sheet. Bake in a preheated 425-degree oven for 15 minutes. Repeat the process with the remaining potato mixture. Cool and freeze in a sealable plastic bag for future use, if desired. Reheat as needed in the microwave or the oven.

Yield: 24 servings

Squash Potato Casserole

6 yellow squash, sliced

4 large potatoes, sliced

1/2 onion, chopped

8 ounces Cheddar cheese, shredded

1/2 cup (1 stick) butter, chopped

3 eggs, beaten

1 sleeve saltine crackers, crushed

Salt and pepper to taste

Nutritional Profiles 230–233

1 Combine the squash, potatoes and onion in a saucepan and add enough water to cover. Bring to a boil and boil until the vegetables are tender; drain.

2 Combine the squash mixture, half the cheese, the butter, eggs, cracker crumbs, salt and pepper in a bowl and mix well.

3 Spoon the squash mixture into a 9×13-inch baking dish and sprinkle with the remaining cheese. Bake in a preheated 375-degree oven for 30 minutes.

Yield: 12 servings

Roasted Squash and Potato Pie

1 bunch green onions, thinly sliced

1 cup (4 ounces) grated Parmesan cheese

2 tablespoons all-purpose flour

1 tablespoon chopped fresh thyme

1/2 teaspoon salt

1/2 teaspoon freshly ground pepper

2 pounds Yukon Gold potatoes, peeled and cut into 1/8-inch-thick slices

12 ounces yellow squash, cut into 1/8-inch-thick slices

6 teaspoons olive oil

Nutritional Profiles 230–233

1 Reserve 1/4 cup of the green onions. Combine the remaining green onions, cheese, flour, thyme, salt and pepper in a bowl and mix well.

2 Coat two 9-inch round baking pans with butter. In each pan layer one-sixth of the potatoes in concentric circles slightly overlapping. Layer one-fourth of the squash in concentric circles over the potatoes. Drizzle each with 1 teaspoon of the olive oil and sprinkle with one-sixth of the cheese mixture. Repeat the process with the potatoes, squash, olive oil and cheese mixture. Top each with half the remaining potatoes, 1 teaspoon of the remaining olive oil and half the remaining cheese mixture and press gently to flatten.

3 Roast, covered with foil, in a preheated 375-degree oven for 40 minutes or until the potatoes are almost tender. Remove the foil and roast for about 25 minutes longer or until the potatoes begin to brown and are tender. Cut each pie into wedges and sprinkle with the reserved 1/4 cup green onions.

4 You may prepare and bake the pies up to 6 hours in advance. Let stand until cool and store, covered with foil, in the refrigerator. Reheat, covered with foil, in a preheated 350-degree oven for about 30 minutes or until heated through.

Yield: 8 servings

Spinach Casserole

2 (10-ounce) packages frozen chopped spinach, thawed and drained

2 cups Pepperidge Farm stuffing mix

1/2 cup (2 ounces) grated Parmesan cheese

1 1/2 teaspoons garlic salt

1 teaspoon pepper

1/4 teaspoon thyme

1/2 cup (1 stick) butter, melted

4 eggs, beaten

Nutritional Profiles 230–233

1 Press any excess moisture from the spinach. Combine the spinach, stuffing mix, cheese, garlic salt, pepper, thyme, butter and eggs in a bowl and mix well.

2 Spoon the spinach mixture into a greased 3- or 4-quart baking dish. Bake in a preheated 350-degree oven for 30 minutes.

3 You may prepare the casserole in advance and store, covered, in the refrigerator. Bake just before serving time, increasing the baking time. Double the recipe for a larger crowd.

Yield: 12 servings

Tomato Zucchini Tian

1 eggplant, peeled

Salt to taste

2 onions, chopped

3 garlic cloves, minced

1/2 cup extra-virgin olive oil

Freshly ground pepper to taste

2 zucchini, diagonally sliced

6 ripe tomatoes, sliced

3 or 4 sprigs of fresh herbs
(thyme, rosemary, oregano)

1/2 cup (2 ounces) grated
Parmigiano-Reggiano cheese

Nutritional Profiles 230–233

1 Chop the eggplant and sprinkle with salt. Drain the eggplant in a colander for 30 minutes; pat dry. Cook the onions and garlic in 3 tablespoons of the olive oil in a medium skillet over medium heat for 10 minutes or until light brown. Remove the onion mixture to a bowl using a slotted spoon, reserving the pan drippings.

2 Heat 2 to 3 tablespoons of the remaining olive oil with the reserved pan drippings and add the eggplant. Cook for 10 minutes or until the eggplant is brown and tender. Season with salt and pepper. Stir the eggplant into the onion mixture.

3 Spoon the eggplant mixture into a baking dish. Layer the zucchini and tomatoes over the prepared layer. Sprinkle with the herbs, drizzle with the remaining olive oil and season with salt and pepper.

4 Bake in a preheated 400-degree oven for 30 to 40 minutes or until light brown and heated through. Sprinkle with the cheese and serve.

Yield: 6 servings

Crescent City Celebrations

New Orleans is a city of celebration, where festivities take place year-round!
We enjoy everything from tailgating parties to holiday, festival, and carnival seasons. With so many events to attend, being mindful of our nutritional intake does not have to be a chore.
What a great reason to create a nutritious and delicious dish together that we can contribute to the party! Of course, there will always be the inevitable treats, and a nibble or two is fine, but remember that other dishes can be just as tasty, too.
In addition, there are many ways to alter popular dishes, appetizers, and desserts to enhance nutritional value. This can be accomplished by reducing fat and/or sugar ingredients. For example, replace high-fat dairy with low-fat or fat-free alternatives. Equal amounts of canola oil may be used in place of melted shortening, butter, or margarine. Sweetness may be achieved with applesauce, reduced-calorie sweeteners, cinnamon, or extracts in place of sugar.
So have a little fun—with creative minds and teamwork, you can cook up a healthy dish worthy of celebration. Kids will be proud to show off a favorite dish they helped to prepare.

Purple Passion Frozen Drink

This healthy, refreshing, and cool drink is especially good on hot summer days.

2 bananas

10 ounces frozen or
fresh strawberries

2 cups orange juice

1 cup ice cubes

Combine the bananas, strawberries, orange juice and ice cubes in a blender.

Process at medium speed until smooth. Pour into glasses and serve immediately.

Yield: 2 servings

Photograph for this recipe on page 130.

Party Punch

3 liters fruit punch

3 liters lemon-lime soda

1/2 gallon strawberry sherbet

Mix 1 liter of the fruit punch and 1 liter of the soda in a pitcher. Pour into a bundt pan and freeze for 8 to 10 hours.

Set the bundt pan in a shallow pan of warm water and let stand until the frozen punch separates from the pan. Invert the frozen ring into a punch bowl and fill the center of the frozen ring with the sherbet.

Pour the remaining fruit punch and the remaining soda around the frozen ring. Ladle into punch cups. The frozen ring will keep the punch cool and will not dilute the punch, and the ladle has a place to rest.

Yield: 24 servings

Witches' Brew

1 gallon cranberry juice, chilled

1 gallon apple cider, chilled

1 (12-ounce) can frozen orange juice concentrate, thawed

Pour the cranberry juice into a punch bowl and add the cider. Stir in the orange juice concentrate. Ladle into punch cups.

For a different effect, add dry ice to the punch bowl. Or, freeze some of the punch in Halloween molds and float in the punch.

Yield: 25 servings

N'awlins Deviled Eggs

12 eggs, hard-cooked

8 ounces pork sausage

1 cup blue cheese salad dressing

1 bunch green onions, chopped

1/2 cup chopped celery

1 teaspoon Creole seasoning

1 teaspoon Creole mustard

Cut the eggs into halves and place the yolks in a bowl. Arrange the whites on a serving platter. Brown the sausage in a skillet, stirring until crumbly; drain.

Add the sausage, salad dressing, green onions, celery, Creole seasoning and Creole mustard to the egg yolks and mix until combined.

Mound the sausage mixture in the egg whites. Serve immediately or store, covered, in the refrigerator.

Yield: 10 to 15 servings

Black Bean Dip

1 (19-ounce) can black beans, drained and rinsed

1/4 cup chopped red bell pepper

2 1/2 tablespoons cider vinegar

1 tablespoon chopped red onion

1 tablespoon chopped cilantro

1 1/2 teaspoons chopped jalapeño chile

1 teaspoon chili powder

Salt and pepper to taste

Combine the beans, bell pepper, vinegar, onion, cilantro, jalapeño chile and chili powder in a blender. Process until puréed. Season with salt and pepper.

Pour the dip into a serving bowl and serve with assorted chips.

Yield: 24 ounces

Mamaw's Chive Dip

16 ounces cream cheese, softened

2 tablespoons mayonnaise

2 tablespoons (or more) finely chopped fresh chives

1 shake of soy sauce

Combine the cream cheese, mayonnaise, chives and soy sauce in a mixing bowl. Beat until combined.

Serve with celery sticks, Doritos tortilla chips and/or party rye bread.

Yield: 8 (1-ounce) servings

Virginia's Jalapeño
Cheese Ball

10 ounces sharp Cheddar
cheese, shredded

8 ounces cream cheese, softened

2 tablespoons chopped
bell pepper

2 tablespoons chopped onion

2 tablespoons chopped
drained pimento

2 teaspoons Worcestershire sauce

2 jalapeño chiles, finely chopped

2 teaspoons jalapeño juice

Dash of garlic powder

Dash of cayenne pepper

Parsley flakes to taste

Chopped pecans

Combine the Cheddar cheese and cream cheese in a mixing
bowl. Beat until combined.

Add the bell pepper, onion, pimento, Worcestershire sauce,
jalapeño chiles, jalapeño juice, garlic powder and cayenne
pepper and mix well. Chill, covered, until firm.

Shape the cheese mixture into two balls and coat with a
mixture of parsley flakes and chopped pecans. Serve with
assorted party crackers.

Yield: 24 ounces

Savory Cheese and
Pimento Appetizer

8 ounces sharp Cheddar
cheese, cut into cubes

8 ounces cream cheese,
cut into cubes

1/2 cup olive oil

1/2 cup white wine vinegar

1 (2-ounce) jar diced pimento

3 tablespoons chopped
fresh parsley

3 tablespoons minced
green onions

3 garlic cloves, minced

1 teaspoon sugar

3/4 teaspoon dried basil

1/2 teaspoon salt

1/2 teaspoon pepper

Arrange the Cheddar cheese cubes and cream cheese cubes
alternately in a shallow serving dish.

Combine the olive oil, vinegar, pimento, parsley, green
onions, garlic, sugar, basil, salt and pepper in a jar with a
tight-fitting lid and seal tightly. Shake to mix.

Pour the olive oil mixture over the cheese cubes. Marinate,
covered, in the refrigerator for 8 hours or longer. Serve with
wooden picks.

Yield: 16 ounces

Photograph for this recipe on page 130.

Cheese Yummies

For younger children, omit the peanuts and serve as a spread with Ritz crackers.

1 (5-ounce) jar Old English
cheese spread

6 ounces cream cheese, softened

1 teaspoon grated onion

1/4 teaspoon cayenne pepper

Dash of garlic salt

Chopped salted peanuts

Combine the cheese spread, cream cheese, onion, cayenne pepper and garlic salt in a bowl and mix well.

Chill, covered, until firm. Shape the cheese mixture into small balls and coat with peanuts.

Yield: 12 ounces

Create enough time at each meal for your family to relax and enjoy the food. Encourage family members to explain what they like to eat and why. **A Crescent City Cutie voices his food preferences:** *"I like to eat healthy foods, and it makes you feel good when beans go in your tummy."*
—McCall Engelhardt

Mardi Gras Salad

Add two pounds chopped cooked chicken for an entrée salad.

Salad

1 head red cabbage, shredded

1 cucumber, peeled and sliced

1 green bell pepper, sliced

1 yellow bell pepper, sliced

1 cup wide chow mein noodles

$1/4$ cup fresh cilantro leaves

$1/2$ cup chopped peanuts

Soy Vinaigrette

$1/2$ cup olive oil

$1/4$ cup soy sauce

$1/4$ cup rice vinegar

2 garlic cloves, minced

2 teaspoons sugar

Pinch of salt

For the salad, toss the cabbage, cucumber, bell peppers, noodles, cilantro and peanuts in a salad bowl.

For the vinaigrette, combine the olive oil, soy sauce, vinegar, garlic, sugar and salt in a jar with a tight-fitting lid and seal tightly. Shake to mix. Add the vinaigrette to the salad and toss to coat.

Yield: 12 servings

Photograph for this recipe on page 130.

LSU Potatoes

Purple potatoes

Shredded Cheddar cheese and/or
mozzarella cheese

Cut potatoes into bite-size pieces. Alternate potatoes and cheese as desired in a baking dish. Bake in a preheated 400-degree oven for 30 minutes or until the potatoes are tender. Stir and serve immediately. Adjust the amounts according to the size of your crowd.

Yield: variable servings

Cheese Grits

1 1/2 cups quick-cooking grits

6 cups water

Salt to taste

16 ounces sharp Cheddar
cheese, shredded

1/2 cup (1 stick) margarine, sliced

2 eggs, beaten

1 teaspoon Worcestershire sauce

1 garlic clove, minced

Combine the grits, water and salt in a saucepan and cook using the package directions. Stir in the cheese, margarine, eggs, Worcestershire sauce and garlic.

Spoon the grits mixture into a baking dish. Bake in a preheated 350-degree oven for about 45 minutes.

You may prepare one day in advance and store, covered, in the refrigerator. Bake just before serving. Double the recipe for a larger crowd. Do not use instant grits.

Yield: 4 servings

Brunch Soufflé

*This is the perfect dish for a brunch. You can prepare it the day before
and then simply pop it in the oven before your guests arrive.*

1/2 cup (1 stick) butter, softened

8 slices white bread,
crusts trimmed

2 cups (8 ounces) shredded sharp
Cheddar cheese

3 cups milk

4 eggs

1 1/2 teaspoons salt

1/2 teaspoon dry mustard

Spread the butter over both sides of the bread. Cover the bottom of a 9×13-inch baking dish with half the bread. Sprinkle with half the cheese and top with the remaining bread. Sprinkle with the remaining cheese.

Whisk the milk, eggs, salt and dry mustard in a bowl until blended. Pour over the prepared layers. Chill, covered, for 24 hours.

Bake, covered, in a preheated 325-degree oven for 30 minutes. Remove the cover and bake for 10 minutes longer or until brown.

Yield: 10 servings

Christmas Morning Pie

A light and easy Christmas breakfast served with sweet rolls or biscuits and fresh fruit. This leaves room for a big Christmas dinner.

1 cup chopped cooked ham

1 cup (4 ounces) shredded Jarlsberg cheese

1/2 bunch green onions, sliced

1/2 cup Bisquick

1 cup milk

2 eggs, lightly beaten

Tony Chachere's Creole seasoning to taste

Sprinkle the ham, cheese and green onions in a greased 9-inch pie plate or 8×8-inch baking pan.

Whisk the baking mix, milk, eggs and Creole seasoning in a bowl until smooth. Pour over the prepared layer.

Bake in a preheated 400-degree oven for 35 to 40 minutes or until light brown. Serve immediately. Double the recipe for a larger crowd.

Yield: 4 servings

*Share in the food preparation process. Whether it be a big one or a little one, everyone gets a job to do. **A Crescent City Cutie describes her favorite kitchen assignment:** "...pushing the buttons on the food processor or using the mixer, because it makes your hands tickle."—Georgia Kate Scott*

Vidalia Onion Pie

1 cup chopped Vidalia onion

1 cup mayonnaise

1 cup (4 ounces) shredded Swiss cheese

Tony Chachere's Creole seasoning to taste

Combine the onion, mayonnaise and cheese in a bowl and mix well. Spread in a 9-inch pie plate.

Bake in a preheated 350-degree oven for 20 to 30 minutes or until bubbly. Sprinkle with Creole seasoning. Serve with toast points.

Yield: 8 to 10 servings

Use your imagination when preparing dishes. There are no rules when it comes to creating new recipes. Just use healthful, fresh ingredients and enjoy yourself. **A unique meal from a Crescent City Cutie:** *"Princess soup. It has a mouse and a princess with a crown in it. If you need a mouse, you can find one in a castle. Put a spoon in and mix and mix until it's done. Then you eat it!"*

—Elizabeth Engelhardt

Grandma Gert's
Orange Biscuits

This is a traditional family Christmas morning breakfast dish. The smell of the orange and cinnamon reminds you of the holidays.

1 (12-ounce) can frozen orange juice concentrate

1 cup sugar

3 tablespoons cornstarch

1 tablespoon cinnamon

3 cups Bisquick

3/4 cup milk

3 tablespoons butter, melted

Cinnamon-sugar to taste

Prepare the orange juice using the package directions, omitting 1/2 can of the water. Whisk 4 cups of the orange juice, 1 cup sugar, the cornstarch and cinnamon in a saucepan until smooth. Bring to a rolling boil over medium-high heat. Reduce the heat and cook for 1 to 2 minutes longer or until thickened and of a sauce consistency, stirring occasionally. Remove from the heat and cover to keep warm.

Mix the baking mix and milk in a bowl until a moist thick dough forms. Sprinkle a hard surface with additional baking mix. Knead the dough on the prepared hard surface about ten times or until the dough is coated and not sticky. Roll the dough into a rectangle 1/2 inch thick. Brush with the butter and sprinkle with cinnamon-sugar.

Roll the rectangle into a roll and cut into 3/4-inch slices. Arrange the rolls cut side up 1/2 inch apart in a 9×13-inch baking dish sprayed with nonstick cooking spray. Pour the orange sauce over the rolls. Bake in a preheated 350-degree oven for 25 minutes. Let stand for a few minutes. To serve, arrange one biscuit on each of twelve serving plates and drizzle evenly with the sauce. Serve warm.

Yield: 12 biscuits

Bercaw Boys' Banana Bread

Allow your children to take turns mashing the bananas and pouring the ingredients into a bowl while munching on walnuts and raisins. This bread is dense, flavorful, and healthful. Full of fruit and fiber with no added fat.

3 bananas

1 cup sugar

1 1/2 cups whole wheat flour

1 teaspoon baking soda

1/2 to 3/4 cup applesauce

1/2 teaspoon vanilla extract

Chopped walnuts (optional)

Raisins (optional)

Mash the bananas in a bowl and stir in the sugar, flour and baking soda.

Stir in the applesauce and vanilla. Mix in walnuts and raisins.

Spoon the batter into a 4×8-inch loaf pan sprayed with butter-flavor nonstick cooking spray. Bake in a preheated 325-degree oven for 1 hour or until a wooden pick inserted in the center comes out clean.

Cool in the pan for 10 minutes. Remove to a wire rack to cool completely.

Yield: 10 slices

Chocolate Chip-Banana Cake

This easy-to-prepare cake makes a great afternoon snack for children and adults.

2 cups all-purpose flour

2 1/2 teaspoons baking powder

1/4 teaspoon salt

1/2 cup (1 stick) butter, softened

1 1/4 cups sugar

2 eggs

1 1/4 cups mashed bananas

1/2 cup evaporated milk

1 teaspoon vanilla extract

1 cup (6 ounces) chocolate chips

Whisk the flour, baking powder and salt in a bowl. Beat the butter and sugar in a mixing bowl until light and fluffy.

Add the eggs to the butter mixture one at a time, beating well after each addition. Beat in the bananas, evaporated milk and vanilla until blended. Whisk in the flour mixture; stir in the chocolate chips.

Spoon the batter into an 8×8-inch cake pan lightly sprayed with nonstick cooking spray. Bake in a preheated 350-degree oven for 55 to 65 minutes or until the cake tests done. Let stand until cool before serving.

Yield: 9 servings

Citrus Yogurt Cake

Very easy to prepare and sweet enough without icing.

I cup all-purpose flour, sifted

1/2 cup plus 2 tablespoons
granulated sugar

1/2 teaspoon baking powder

1/2 teaspoon baking soda

Pinch of salt

1/2 cup plain low-fat yogurt

1/4 cup vegetable oil

I tablespoon orange juice

I teaspoon grated orange zest

1/2 teaspoon grated lemon zest

I egg

1/2 teaspoon vanilla extract

Unsalted butter

Confectioners' sugar to taste

Whisk the flour, granulated sugar, baking powder, baking soda and salt in a bowl. Add the yogurt, oil, orange juice, orange zest, lemon zest, egg and vanilla and stir until combined.

Coat an 8-inch cake pan with unsalted butter. Spread the batter in the prepared pan. Bake in a preheated 350-degree oven for 25 minutes or until a wooden pick inserted in the center comes out clean.

Cool in the pan for 10 minutes. Remove to a wire rack to cool completely. Dust with confectioners' sugar before serving.

Yield: 6 to 8 servings

King Cake for Kids1 (16-ounce) can Grands biscuits
1/4 cup (1/2 stick) butter, melted
1/4 cup sugar
1 tablespoon cinnamon
1 small plastic baby (optional)
1 can cream cheese frosting
Yellow, green and purple sprinkles

Line a baking sheet with foil. Place the biscuit dough on the prepared baking sheet and pat into a circle. Brush the dough with the butter and sprinkle with the sugar and cinnamon. Add the plastic baby.

Roll the dough into a cylinder and shape into a ring by bringing the two ends together. Pinch the ends to seal.

Bake in a preheated 325-degree oven for 35 minutes. Let stand until warm.

Lightly spread the frosting over the top and side of the warm cake and top with sprinkles.

Yield: 12 servings

Photograph for this recipe on page 130.

It's OK to splurge sometimes. Holidays and special occasions often involve more decadent dishes and desserts. When celebrating, just be aware of portion size and choose only one or two things in which to indulge, not the whole array of options. **A Crescent City Cutie shares her favorite way to celebrate:** "Eat cake!"

—Olivia Elizabeth Zeller O'Bell

Sally's Mandarin Orange-
Pineapple Cake

Cake

1 (2-layer) package Betty Crocker
moist yellow cake mix

4 eggs

3/4 cup canola oil

1 (11-ounce) can mandarin
oranges

Pineapple Frosting

1 (15-ounce) can juice-pack
crushed pineapple

2 (4-ounce) packages vanilla
instant pudding mix

16 ounces Cool Whip
whipped topping

For the cake, combine the cake mix, eggs, canola oil and undrained mandarin oranges in a mixing bowl and beat for 2 minutes. Spread the batter evenly in three greased and floured 9-inch cake pans.

Bake in a preheated 350-degree oven for 15 to 20 minutes or until wooden picks inserted in the centers come out clean. Cool in the pans for 10 minutes. Remove to a wire rack to cool completely.

For the frosting, combine the undrained pineapple, pudding mix and whipped topping in a mixing bowl. Beat at low speed until combined.

Spread the frosting between the layers and over the top and side of the cake. Store, covered, in the refrigerator.

Yield: 12 servings

Pineapple Goo Cake

Cake

2 cups all-purpose flour

2 cups sugar

1 teaspoon baking soda

1/4 teaspoon salt

2 (8-ounce) cans
crushed pineapple

2 eggs

1 teaspoon vanilla extract

Icing and Assembly

1 1/2 cups sugar

1 cup (2 sticks) butter

1 (5-ounce) can evaporated milk

1 teaspoon vanilla extract

1 cup chopped pecans or
nuts of choice

1 cup sweetened flaked coconut

For the cake, whisk the flour, sugar, baking soda and salt in a mixing bowl. Add the undrained pineapple, eggs and vanilla and beat at medium speed until combined. Spread the batter in a lightly greased and floured 9×13-inch cake pan.

Bake in a preheated 350-degree oven for 30 minutes or until a wooden pick inserted in the center comes out clean.

For the frosting, bring the sugar, butter and evaporated milk to a boil in a saucepan over medium heat. Boil for 2 minutes, stirring constantly. Remove from the heat and stir in the vanilla.

Make 1/2-inch-deep holes at 1-inch intervals in the top of the warm cake. Pour the frosting evenly over the warm cake and sprinkle with the pecans and coconut. Let stand until cool and then cut into squares. Store, covered, in the refrigerator.

Yield: 15 servings

Great-Grandmother's
Red Velvet Cake

Cake

2 1/2 cups sifted all-purpose flour

2 tablespoons baking cocoa

1 teaspoon salt

1/2 cup (1 stick) butter
or shortening

1 cup sugar

2 eggs

2 ounces red food coloring

1 cup buttermilk

1 teaspoon vanilla extract

1 tablespoon vinegar

1 teaspoon Arm & Hammer
baking soda

Red Velvet Icing

1 cup milk

1/4 cup all-purpose flour

1 cup Crisco

1 cup sugar

1 teaspoon vanilla extract

For the cake, sift the flour, baking cocoa and salt into a bowl and mix well. Beat the butter, sugar and eggs in a mixing bowl until creamy. Add the food coloring and beat until blended. Add the flour mixture alternately with the buttermilk, beating constantly at medium speed until blended after each addition. Mix in the vanilla. Stir in the vinegar and baking soda with a wooden spoon. Spread the batter in two greased 8-inch cake pans.

Bake in a preheated 350-degree oven for 30 minutes. Cool in the pans for 10 minutes. Remove to a wire rack to cool completely.

For the icing, whisk the milk and flour in a saucepan until blended. Cook over low heat until the consistency of pudding. Remove from the heat and let stand until cool.

Beat the shortening and sugar in a mixing bowl at high speed until light and fluffy. Add the milk mixture and vanilla and beat to the desired consistency. You cannot overbeat the icing. Spread the icing between the layers and over the top and side of the cake. Store, covered, in the refrigerator. Leftover icing should also be stored in the refrigerator.

For variety, bake in three cake pans and spread with your favorite cream cheese frosting.

Yield: 12 servings

Microwave Pralines

Sorry, Grandma, I do not have the time to spend stirring!

1 (1-pound) package light
brown sugar

1 cup whipping cream

1 1/2 cups pecans

2 tablespoons butter

1 teaspoon vanilla extract

Combine the brown sugar and cream in a microwave-safe bowl and mix well. Microwave on High for 12 to 13 minutes. Stir in the pecans, butter and vanilla.

Drop by teaspoonfuls onto a sheet of waxed paper. Let stand until firm. Store in an airtight container.

Yield: about 30 pralines

Lisa's Peanut Butter Squares

1 1/2 cups (3 sticks) butter or
margarine, melted

8 ounces graham cracker crumbs

4 cups confectioners' sugar

2 cups peanut butter

1 package milk chocolate chips

Combine the butter, graham cracker crumbs, confectioners' sugar and peanut butter in a bowl and mix well. Pat over the bottom of a buttered 9×13-inch baking pan.

Place the chocolate chips in a microwave-safe bowl and microwave until melted. Spread over the prepared layer.

Chill, covered, until set. Serve at room temperature or slightly chilled. Store in an airtight container.

Yield: 3 to 4 dozen squares

Pumpkin Squares

Squares

2 cups all-purpose flour

2 teaspoons baking powder

2 teaspoons cinnamon

1 teaspoon baking soda

1 teaspoon salt

4 eggs

2 cups sugar

1 (16-ounce) can pumpkin

1 cup vegetable oil

Cream Cheese Icing

3 ounces cream cheese, softened

1/4 cup (1/2 stick)
butter, softened

3 1/2 cups confectioners' sugar

1 tablespoon water

1 teaspoon vanilla extract

For the squares, whisk the flour, baking powder, cinnamon, baking soda and salt in a bowl. Beat the eggs in a mixing bowl until blended. Add the sugar, pumpkin, oil and flour mixture and beat until combined. Spread the batter in a 10×15-inch baking pan sprayed with nonstick cooking spray.

Bake in a preheated 350-degree oven for 20 to 25 minutes or until a wooden pick inserted in the center comes out clean. Let stand until cool and then cut into 1×2-inch squares.

For the icing, beat the cream cheese and butter in a mixing bowl until creamy. Add the confectioners' sugar, water and vanilla and beat until of a spreading consistency. Top each square with a tablespoon of the icing.

Yield: 4 dozen squares

Coconut Macaroons

4 cups shredded coconut

1/2 cup all-purpose flour

1 1/3 cups sweetened
condensed milk

2 teaspoons vanilla extract

Mix the coconut and flour in a bowl. Add the condensed milk and vanilla and stir with a wooden spoon until combined. Drop by teaspoonfuls 2 inches apart onto a greased cookie sheet.

Bake in a preheated 325-degree oven for 15 minutes or until golden brown. Remove to a wire rack to cool. Store in an airtight container.

Yield: about 40 macaroons

Lace Oatmeal Cookies

1/2 cup (1 stick) butter, melted

1 cup old-fashioned oats

1 cup sugar

1 egg, lightly beaten

1 1/2 teaspoons all-purpose flour

1/2 teaspoon vanilla extract

Pour the butter over the oats in a bowl and mix well. Let stand for 15 minutes. Combine the sugar, egg, flour and vanilla in a bowl and mix well. Stir in the oats mixture.

Drop the oats mixture by teaspoonfuls 2 inches apart onto a cookie sheet lined with foil. Bake in a preheated 325-degree oven for 12 to 14 minutes or until golden brown.

Let stand until cool and then peel the cookies off the foil. Store in an airtight container. You may reuse the same sheet of foil for the entire batch of cookies.

Yield: 5 dozen cookies

Melting Moments

Cookies

3/4 cup (1 1/2 sticks) butter

1/4 cup confectioners' sugar

1 cup all-purpose flour

1/4 cup cornstarch

Butter Frosting

1/4 cup (1/2 stick) butter

1/4 cup confectioners' sugar

1/2 teaspoon vanilla extract

For the cookies, beat the butter and confectioners' sugar in a mixing bowl until creamy. Add the flour and cornstarch and beat until blended. Drop the dough by half teaspoonfuls onto a greased cookie sheet.

Bake in a preheated 350-degree oven for 10 to 15 minutes or until light brown. Cool on the cookie sheet for 2 minutes. Remove to a wire rack to cool completely.

For the frosting, beat the butter, confectioners' sugar and vanilla in a mixing bowl until of a spreading consistency. Spread the frosting over the tops of the cookies. Store in an airtight container.

Yield: 2 dozen

Magical Mocha Wands

1 cup (2 sticks) butter
(no substitutes)

3/4 cup sugar

4 teaspoons instant espresso
coffee powder

1/2 teaspoon salt

1/4 teaspoon baking powder

1 egg

1 teaspoon vanilla extract

1 1/3 cups all-purpose flour

8 ounces semisweet chocolate,
melted and cooled

1 1/2 cups finely chopped pecans

Beat the butter in a mixing bowl for 30 seconds. Add the sugar, coffee powder, salt and baking powder and beat until blended. Mix in the egg and vanilla. Beat in as much of the flour as possible and stir in the remaining flour.

Press the dough into 3-inch strips using a cookie press fitted with a star plate or use a pastry bag fitted with a star tip. Arrange the strips on an ungreased cookie sheet.

Bake in a preheated 375-degree oven for 10 to 12 minutes or until light brown. Cool on the cookie sheet for 2 minutes. Remove to a wire rack to cool completely.

Dip the ends of the cookies in the chocolate and sprinkle with the pecans. Let stand until set. Store in an airtight container.

Yield: 6 dozen cookies

Baby Fingers

1 loaf sliced white bread, crusts trimmed

8 ounces cream cheese, softened

1 (8-ounce) can crushed pineapple, drained

2 cups sugar

1/2 cup cinnamon

1 cup (2 sticks) margarine, melted

Flatten the bread slices as thin as possible on a hard surface using a rolling pin. Beat the cream cheese and pineapple in a mixing bowl until combined. Spread 1 tablespoon of the cream cheese mixture on one side of each slice of bread. Roll to enclose the filling and cut the rolls into halves.

Mix the sugar and cinnamon in a shallow dish. Dip each roll in the margarine and coat with the cinnamon-sugar. Arrange on an ungreased cookie sheet. Bake in a preheated 350-degree oven for 10 to 12 minutes or until light brown. Cool on the cookie sheet for 2 minutes. Remove to a wire rack to cool completely. Store in an airtight container.

Yield: 4 dozen

Banana Caramel Pie

2 (14-ounce) cans sweetened condensed milk

1 1/2 cups pecans, toasted

1 baked (9-inch) pie shell or graham cracker pie shell

2 bananas, sliced

8 ounces Cool Whip whipped topping

Pour the condensed milk into a pie plate and cover with foil. Place the pie plate in a baking pan and add enough hot water to come halfway up the side of the pie plate. Bake in a preheated 425-degree oven for 1 hour or until thick and caramel colored.

Sprinkle the pecans over the bottom of the pie shell and pour the hot caramel over the prepared layer. Layer with the bananas and spread with the whipped topping. Serve warm or chilled.

Yield: 6 to 8 servings

Microwave Chocolate Pie

Pie

1 cup sugar

3 tablespoons baking cocoa

3 tablespoons cornstarch

2 cups milk

3 egg yolks

3 tablespoons margarine

1 teaspoon vanilla extract

1 baked (9-inch) pie shell

Meringue

4 egg whites

1/2 teaspoon cream of tartar

1/2 cup sugar

1 teaspoon vanilla extract

For the pie, combine the sugar, baking cocoa and cornstarch in a microwave-safe bowl and mix well. Add the milk and stir until smooth. Microwave on High for 2 minutes.

Beat the egg yolks in a mixing bowl until blended. Stir a small amount of the hot milk mixture into the egg yolks. Stir the egg yolks into the hot milk mixture.

Microwave on High for 4 to 5 minutes or until thickened. Add the margarine and vanilla and stir until the margarine melts. Pour the filling into the pie shell.

For the meringue, beat the egg whites and cream of tartar in a mixing bowl until frothy. Add the sugar gradually, beating constantly until stiff peaks form. Fold in the vanilla. Spread the meringue over the filling, sealing to the edge.

Bake in a preheated 350-degree oven for 8 to 10 minutes or until light brown. Serve chilled.

Yield: 6 to 8 servings

Pecan Pie

4 cups pecans

2 unbaked (9-inch) pie shells

5 eggs

2 cups sugar

1 cup Karo light corn syrup

1/2 cup (1 stick) margarine, melted

Sprinkle 2 cups of the pecans in each pie shell. Beat the eggs in a mixing bowl until blended. Add the sugar and corn syrup and beat until combined. Beat in the margarine.

Pour equal portions of the syrup mixture into each pie shell. Bake in a preheated 325-degree oven for 1 hour or until the center is firm. Cool on a wire rack.

Yield: 6 to 8 servings

Pink Lemonade Pie

1 (14-ounce) can sweetened condensed milk

1 (12-ounce) can frozen pink lemonade concentrate

8 ounces Cool Whip whipped topping

1 graham cracker pie shell

Beat the condensed milk, lemonade concentrate and whipped topping in a mixing bowl until blended.

Spread the filling in the pie shell. Freeze until firm. Serve frozen.

Yield: 6 to 8 servings

Million Dollar Pie

3 kiwifruit, chopped

2 bananas, sliced

1 (8-ounce) can crushed pineapple, drained

1 (4-ounce) jar maraschino cherries, drained and chopped

1 cup pecans, chopped

1 cup grated coconut

12 ounces Cool Whip whipped topping

1 (14-ounce) can sweetened condensed milk

1/4 cup lemon juice

2 graham cracker pie shells

Combine the kiwifruit, bananas, pineapple, cherries, pecans and coconut in a bowl and mix well. Stir in the whipped topping, condensed milk and lemon juice.

Spoon half the filling into each pie shell. Chill for 30 minutes or longer.

Yield: 12 to 16 servings

Set rules when it comes to sweet treats. Be clear regarding how much and how often these can be consumed. Don't forget to offer healthful foods as treats as well. Try to dispel the notion that only the sweet foods are considered "treats." **A healthy eating tip from a Crescent City Cutie:** *"Never have more than one treat a day unless you are at Grandmother Pat Pat's."*

—*Gabrielle Schwarz*

Crescent City Cultures

The history of our city is rich with many different cultures and ethnic backgrounds. In present-day New Orleans one can find wholesome and delicious dishes from a great many of the world's countries. These cultures enjoy dishes with fresh, natural ingredients, including spices that may have significant health benefits. Some widely used ethnic spices are turmeric (found in curry powder), cumin, dill, cloves, ginger, and fennel. Studies have shown that these herbs and spices have antioxidant properties, may block carcinogens, and boost immune function. Try a sprinkle of some of these spices on your favorite dishes for added flavor and health benefits. Exposing children to different types of foods from other countries will not only broaden their taste buds but will broaden their minds as well. Kids can have a chance to understand other cultures, enriching their perspective on different heritages. So, go ahead and experiment and explore different dishes. You may find some new favorites along the way!

Tzatziki

1 large cucumber

3/4 cup plain yogurt

3/4 cup sour cream

3 tablespoons olive oil

3 garlic cloves, minced

4 1/2 teaspoons minced fresh dill weed

4 1/2 teaspoons red wine vinegar

1/4 teaspoon salt

Peel the cucumber and cut lengthwise into halves. Scoop out the seeds and discard. Grate the cucumber. Squeeze the grated cucumber between paper towels to remove any excess moisture.

Combine the cucumber, yogurt, sour cream, olive oil, garlic, dill weed, vinegar and salt in a serving bowl and mix well.

Chill, covered, in the refrigerator. Garnish with additional minced dill weed and serve with pita wedges.

Yield: 24 ounces

Greek

Guacamole

A good guacamole tastes best when you can actually taste the chunky avocado.
Minimal seasoning is needed to bring out the delicious flavor.

3 small or medium ripe avocados

1 teaspoon lemon juice

1/2 teaspoon garlic salt

1/2 teaspoon pepper

1/2 small tomato, chopped

2 tablespoons minced onion

1 tablespoon mayonnaise or sour cream (optional)

Tex-Mex

Mash the avocados in a bowl to the desired consistency using a fork. Stir in the lemon juice, garlic salt and pepper.

Add the tomato and onion and mix just until combined. Stir in the mayonnaise. Serve immediately with tortilla chips. Adding mayonnaise or sour cream increases the creaminess of the guacamole.

Yield: 10 (1/4-cup) servings

Making recipes with children also helps create fond memories to last a lifetime. Relax, forget the daily stresses, and have fun while you cook. **A Crescent City Cutie shares his joy in helping prepare dinner:** *"I like to pour the rice in the pan. It sounds cool, like rain."*

—Chaz Bregman

Italian Wedding Soup

8 ounces extra-lean ground beef

1 egg, lightly beaten

2 tablespoon dry bread crumbs

1 tablespoon grated
Parmesan cheese

1/2 teaspoon dried basil

1/2 teaspoon onion powder

53/4 cups chicken broth

2 cups thinly sliced escarole

1 cup orzo

1/3 cup finely chopped carrots

Italian

Combine the ground beef, egg, bread crumbs, cheese, basil and onion powder in a bowl and mix well. Shape into 3/4-inch balls.

Bring the broth to a rolling boil in a saucepan. Add the meatballs, escarole, pasta and carrots to the broth. Return the broth to a boil; reduce the heat to medium.

Cook for 10 minutes or until the pasta is al dente, stirring frequently. Ladle into soup bowls.

Yield: 4 servings

Sesame Sweet-and-Tangy
Cucumbers

3 cucumbers

1 tablespoon salt

1/4 cup sugar

1/4 cup white vinegar

1 garlic clove, minced or crushed

1 teaspoon sesame oil

1 teaspoon (or more)
sesame seeds

Cut the cucumbers into 1/8- to 1/4-inch slices. Place the slices in a serving bowl and sprinkle with the salt. Let stand for 30 minutes; drain. Rinse the cucumbers under cold water and drain again.

Mix the sugar, vinegar, garlic and sesame oil in a bowl. Add the cucumber slices and stir until coated. Return the cucumber mixture to the serving bowl.

Chill for 30 minutes. Sprinkle with the sesame seeds just before serving.

Yield: 8 servings

Photograph for this recipe on page 162.

Couscous Salad

1 (6-ounce) package chicken-
flavor couscous

1 (6-ounce) package cooked
chicken strips, chopped

6 ounces feta cheese, crumbled

2 Roma tomatoes, chopped, or
6 sun-dried tomatoes, chopped

1/2 cup shredded carrots

3 green onions, sliced

1/4 cup vinaigrette

Moroccan

Cook the couscous using the package directions, omitting the oil. Combine the chicken, cheese, tomatoes, carrots and green onions in a bowl and mix well.

Stir in the couscous. Add the vinaigrette and toss to coat.

Yield: 5 servings

Honey's Hungarian Goulash

Goulash

2 pounds beef chuck

$1/2$ teaspoon salt

2 white or yellow onions, chopped

2 tablespoons shortening

2 tablespoons Hungarian
sweet paprika

2 bay leaves

4 cups water

4 potatoes, peeled and chopped

$1/2$ teaspoon salt

$1/4$ teaspoon pepper

Egg Dumplings and Assembly

6 tablespoons all-purpose flour

$1/8$ teaspoon salt

I egg

For the goulash, cut the beef into 1-inch pieces and season with $1/2$ teaspoon salt. Brown the onions in the shortening in a Dutch oven. Add the beef, paprika and bay leaves and mix well.

Simmer over low heat for I hour, stirring occasionally. Stir in the water, potatoes, $1/2$ teaspoon salt and the pepper. Simmer, covered, until the potatoes and beef are tender, stirring occasionally.

For the dumplings, add the flour and salt to the unbeaten egg in a bowl and mix well. Let stand for 30 minutes to allow the flour to mellow.

Drop the batter by teaspoonfuls into the goulash. Simmer, covered, for 5 minutes or until the dumplings rise to the surface. Discard the bay leaves. Serve hot with dollops of sour cream. Use Hungarian paprika for ultimate flavor.

Yield: 6 servings

Sauerbraten

1 cup cider vinegar

1 cup water

1 tablespoon salt

6 whole cloves

6 peppercorns

2 bay leaves

1 (4-pound) beef rump roast,
fat trimmed

1 large onion, cut into halves and
thinly sliced

1 cup crushed gingersnaps
(18 to 20 cookies)

German

Combine the vinegar, water, salt, cloves, peppercorns and bay leaves in a 3½-quart slow cooker or large bowl and mix well. Add the beef and onion. Marinate, covered, in the refrigerator for 1 to 2 days, stirring occasionally.

Discard 1 cup of the marinade. Cook the beef mixture, covered, on Low for 7 to 9 hours or until the beef is tender. Remove the beef to a cutting board and cover to keep warm, reserving the juices in the slow cooker.

Discard the cloves, peppercorns and bay leaves from the reserved juices. Add the gingersnap crumbs to the reserved juices and stir until the crumbs dissolve.

Cook, covered, on High for 15 minutes or until thickened. Slice the beef across the grain and serve with the gingersnap gravy.

Yield: 8 to 10

Bobotie

2 tablespoons vegetable oil

2 onions, minced

1 1/2 pounds ground beef

1 cup milk

2 slices thick-cut Texas toast

1/2 cup raisins

1 tablespoon hot chutney

1 1/2 teaspoons curry powder

1 teaspoon apricot jam

1 teaspoon salt

1/2 teaspoon pepper

1 egg

Pinch of salt

1 bay leaf

African

Heat the oil in a large skillet over medium-high heat. Add the onions to the hot oil and cook until the onions are tender. Add the ground beef to the skillet and cook until the beef is brown and crumbly, stirring frequently; drain.

Pour the milk into a shallow dish. Soak the bread in the milk until saturated. Squeeze any excess milk from the bread into the remaining milk and reserve.

Add the bread to the ground beef mixture and mix well. Stir in the raisins, chutney, curry powder, jam, 1 teaspoon salt and the pepper.

Spoon the ground beef mixture into a lightly greased 9×13-inch baking dish. Bake in a preheated 350-degree oven for 1 hour. Maintain the oven temperature.

Whisk the reserved milk, egg and a pinch of salt in a bowl until blended. Pour over the baked layer and arrange the bay leaf on the top. Bake for 25 to 30 minutes or until golden brown. Discard the bay leaf before serving.

Yield: 4 servings

Grandma's Swedish Meatballs

Meatballs

4 slices white bread

$1/2$ cup milk

2 eggs

1 pound ground beef

3 tablespoons grated
Parmesan cheese

1 teaspoon parsley flakes

$1/4$ teaspoon dried oregano, crushed

1 teaspoon salt

Dash of pepper

$1/3$ cup vegetable oil

For the meatballs, tear the bread into small pieces and place in a bowl. Pour the milk over the bread and let soak for several minutes or until saturated, stirring occasionally. Add the eggs and beat until combined.

Combine the ground beef, cheese, parsley flakes, oregano, salt and pepper in a bowl and mix well. Add the bread mixture and mix well.

Shape the ground beef mixture into 1- to $1 1/2$-inch balls. Sauté the meatballs in the oil in a large skillet until brown on all sides. Remove the meatballs to a bowl using a slotted spoon. Discard the pan drippings.

Creamy Meatball Sauce and Assembly

3 tablespoons salted butter

1/4 cup all-purpose flour

1 (10-ounce) can beef broth

1/2 cup half-and-half

Salt and pepper to taste

1/4 teaspoon dill weed

8 to 16 ounces Mrs. Grass fine egg noodles, cooked and drained

For the sauce, melt the butter in the same skillet over low heat. Whisk in the flour and cook for several minutes or until the mixture is glossy; do not allow the flour to brown. Whisk in the broth and half-and-half.

Cook until thick and satiny, stirring constantly. Season with salt and pepper and stir in the dill weed.

Add the meatballs to the sauce and simmer for 10 minutes, stirring occasionally. Spoon the sauce and meatballs over the hot cooked noodles on a serving platter.

Yield: 6 to 8 servings

Bigos

The secret of Bigos is that the flavor improves each time it is reheated.

1 pound pork loin chops or pork ribs

1 pound spareribs

1 pound smoked pork

1 cup water

4 pounds sauerkraut

1 cup apple juice

4 pounds cabbage, finely chopped

2 bay leaves

Salt and pepper to taste

4 ounces bacon

2 tablespoons all-purpose flour

1/2 cup chopped onion

10 ounces fresh mushrooms

6 ounces dried mushrooms

1 pound smoked kielbasa, sliced

1 (28-ounce) can tomatoes

1 cup water

Brown the pork chops and spareribs in a large stockpot. Add the smoked pork and 1 cup water and simmer for 1 hour. Add the sauerkraut, apple juice and cabbage. Add the bay leaves and season heavily with salt and pepper.

Simmer, covered, for 1 hour. Remove the cover and reduce the heat to a very low simmer. Fry the bacon in a skillet until very crisp. Remove the bacon to a platter, reserving the bacon drippings. Crumble the bacon into the sauerkraut mixture.

Discard most of the reserved bacon drippings. Whisk the flour into the remaining bacon drippings until blended. Stir in the onion and mushrooms. Cook just until the onion and mushrooms begin to brown, stirring frequently. Stir into the sauerkraut mixture. Add the kielbasa, tomatoes and 1 cup water and bring to a boil. Reduce the heat.

Simmer for 30 minutes, stirring occasionally. Discard the bay leaves. Serve hot with French bread.

Yield: 12 servings

Polish

Arroz con Pollo

1/4 cup vegetable oil

1 chicken, cut up

1 1/2 cups water

1 cup chopped celery

1 green bell pepper, chopped

1 cup long grain rice

1 (8-ounce) can tomato sauce

1/2 cup chopped onion

1 garlic clove, minced

2 teaspoons salt

1/2 teaspoon pepper

1/4 to 1/2 teaspoon
crumbled saffron

Spanish

Heat the oil in a large heavy skillet over medium heat. Add the chicken to the hot oil and cook until the chicken is brown on all sides. Remove the chicken to a bowl using a slotted spoon, reserving 2 tablespoons of the pan drippings.

Add the water, celery, bell pepper, rice, tomato sauce, onion, garlic, salt, pepper and saffron to the reserved pan drippings and mix well. Return the chicken to the skillet.

Cook, covered, over low heat for 30 to 40 minutes or until the rice is tender and the chicken is cooked through.

Yield: 4 to 6 servings

Coq au Vin

8 ounces pancetta, chopped

1 chicken, cooked and chopped

$1/2$ teaspoon salt

$1/2$ teaspoon pepper

2 tablespoons olive oil

2 carrots, sliced

2 onions, minced or chopped

1 shallot, sliced

2 garlic cloves, chopped

2 tablespoons all-purpose flour

$2^1/2$ cups burgundy

$1^1/2$ tablespoons Cognac

8 ounces mushrooms, sliced

6 pearl onions

1 bay leaf

1 teaspoon thyme

1 teaspoon salt

$1/4$ teaspoon peppercorns, ground

6 to 12 red potatoes, peeled and cooked

2 tablespoons chopped parsley

Cook the pancetta in a large skillet until brown. Remove the pancetta to a plate using a slotted spoon, reserving the pan drippings.

Add the chicken to the reserved pan drippings and sauté until golden brown on all sides. Sprinkle with $1/2$ teaspoon salt and the pepper. Remove the chicken to a plate, reserving the pan drippings.

Add the olive oil, carrots, minced onions, shallot and garlic to the reserved pan drippings.

Cook until the carrots and onions are tender. Add the flour, stirring constantly until combined. Mix in the wine, brandy, pancetta and chicken. Stir in the mushrooms, pearl onions, bay leaf, thyme, 1 teaspoon salt and the ground peppercorns.

Simmer, covered, over low heat for 1 hour. Discard the bay leaf. Arrange equal portions of the chicken and potatoes on each of six serving plates. Drizzle with the sauce and sprinkle with the parsley.

Yield: 6 servings

French

Grandpa Pablo's Fideos con Pollo

1 chicken

1 bay leaf

1/2 teaspoon ground cumin

1/2 teaspoon garlic powder

1/2 teaspoon salt

3 tablespoons vegetable oil

5 ounces fideos (Spanish pasta)

1/2 cup chopped onion

2 large tomatoes

2 garlic cloves, minced

1 1/2 teaspoons salt

1/8 teaspoon ground cumin

1 bell pepper, finely chopped

Tex-Mex

Combine the chicken, bay leaf, 1/2 teaspoon cumin, the garlic powder and 1/2 teaspoon salt with enough water to cover in a stockpot. Bring to a boil and boil until the chicken is cooked through and very tender.

Remove the chicken to a platter, reserving 4 cups of the stock. Chop the chicken into medium to large pieces, discarding the skin and bones.

Heat the oil in a large skillet and add the pasta. Sauté until the pasta is golden brown, stirring occasionally. Add the onion and sauté for 2 minutes. Remove from the heat.

Process the tomatoes, garlic cloves, 1 1/2 teaspoons salt and 1/8 teaspoon cumin in a blender until puréed. Add the purée and bell pepper to the pasta mixture and simmer for 5 minutes. Stir in the reserved 4 cups stock and chicken.

Simmer, covered, for 20 minutes or until the pasta is tender, adding water as needed if the mixture becomes too dry. You may substitute canned chicken broth for the chicken stock, if desired.

Yield: 4 to 6 servings

Jerk Chicken

1 cup orange juice

1 cup white vinegar

1/2 cup olive oil

1/2 cup soy sauce

3 onions, finely chopped

6 Scotch bonnet chiles or jalapeño chiles, sliced

8 garlic cloves, finely chopped

Juice of 1 lime

2 tablespoons thyme

2 tablespoons ground allspice

2 tablespoons sugar

2 tablespoons salt

2 teaspoons pepper

2 teaspoons cinnamon

2 teaspoons nutmeg

2 teaspoons ginger

3 1/2 pounds chicken pieces, cut into serving pieces

Combine the orange juice, vinegar, olive oil, soy sauce, onions, Scotch bonnet chiles and garlic in a blender. Add the lime juice, thyme, allspice, sugar, salt, pepper, cinnamon, nutmeg and ginger and process until of a sauce consistency.

Reserve some of the sauce to serve with the chicken. Store the reserved sauce in the refrigerator. Bring to room temperature before serving.

Rub some of the remaining sauce over the chicken pieces and arrange in a shallow baking dish. Marinate, covered, in the refrigerator for 8 to 10 hours.

Bake in a preheated 400-degree oven for 1 hour, turning the chicken halfway through the baking process and basting with the remaining sauce. Serve with the reserved sauce.

Yield: 4 to 5 servings

Jamaican

Adobo

2 pounds chicken wings

3 tablespoons vegetable oil

¹/₂ teaspoon salt

¹/₂ teaspoon pepper

¹/₂ onion, sliced and
cut into quarters

2 garlic cloves, minced

¹/₂ cup vinegar

¹/₂ cup soy sauce

2 tablespoons parsley flakes

¹/₂ teaspoon sage

4 cups water

2 cups rice

Philippine

Fry the chicken in the oil in a skillet until brown and crisp. Sprinkle with the salt and pepper. Add the onion and garlic and cook for 8 minutes. Stir in the vinegar, soy sauce, parsley flakes and sage.

Reduce the heat and simmer, covered, for 20 to 30 minutes or until the chicken is cooked through.

Bring the water to a boil in a saucepan and stir in the rice. Boil for 2 minutes. Reduce the heat and simmer, covered, for 20 minutes.

Arrange the chicken over the rice on a serving platter. You may substitute any meat for the chicken.

Yield: 6 to 8 servings

Photograph for this recipe on page 162.

Asian Sugar Snap Peas

This is a great recipe for teens and/or parents with younger children to prepare together. A great accompaniment to meat loaf, pork loin, or chicken, it is a simple introduction to some basic Asian ingredients.

1/2 cup soy sauce

2 tablespoons hoisin sauce

1 tablespoon cornstarch

1 tablespoon minced fresh ginger

2 teaspoons chili garlic sauce

1 teaspoon pepper

1 pound sugar snap peas, trimmed

1/2 cup water

Whisk the soy sauce, hoisin sauce, cornstarch, ginger, chili garlic sauce and pepper in a bowl until combined. Heat a large skillet or wok over medium heat and add the peas and water.

Steam, covered, to the desired degree of crispness, stirring occasionally. Reduce the heat and stir in the soy sauce mixture. Cook over low heat until thickened, stirring frequently.

Yield: 5 servings

Photograph for this recipe on page 162.

Asian

Crash Hot Potatoes

10 new potatoes

Kosher salt to taste

3 tablespoons olive oil

Pepper to taste

Rosemary to taste

Australian

Cook the potatoes in boiling salted water in a large saucepan until tender; drain. Coat the bottom of a 10×15-inch baking pan or baking sheet with sides with some of the olive oil. Arrange the potatoes 1 1/2 inches apart in the prepared pan.

Slightly mash each potato to resemble a cookie using a potato masher. Brush the tops with the remaining olive oil and season generously with salt, pepper and rosemary.

Bake on the top rack in a preheated 450-degree oven for 20 to 25 minutes or until golden brown and crisp. Serve immediately.

Yield: 5 servings

Saag Paneer

Do not let the number of ingredients in this recipe intimidate you. Children can help measure the spices, and the recipe exposes them to spices uncommon in the American diet in a tasty way. This is a terrific meatless meal.

Rice

4 cups water

2 cups basmati rice

1 teaspoon canola oil

Pinch of sea salt

Spinach and Cheese

5 tablespoons canola oil

4 garlic cloves, pressed

1/2 teaspoon cumin seeds

1 onion, chopped

1 (4-ounce) can green chiles

1 teaspoon curry powder

4 bay leaves

For the rice, combine the water, rice, canola oil and salt in a 3-quart saucepan. Let stand for 15 minutes. Bring to a boil over high heat. Reduce the heat to low and cook for 15 to 20 minutes or until the rice is tender. Cover to keep warm.

For the spinach and cheese, heat a wok or deep skillet over medium heat and pour in the canola oil. Stir in the garlic and cumin seeds. Cook for 1 to 2 minutes or until golden brown, stirring constantly. Add the onion, green chiles, curry powder and bay leaves and mix well.

1 (14-ounce) package frozen chopped spinach, thawed

1 teaspoon turmeric

1 teaspoon chili powder

1 teaspoon garam masala

1 teaspoon coriander

Pinch of sea salt

2 vine-ripe tomatoes, chopped

8 ounces paneer cheese, cut into cubes

1/2 to 3/4 cup half-and-half

1/2 to 3/4 cup milk

Cook for 5 minutes or until the onion is tender, stirring occasionally. Stir in the spinach, turmeric, chili powder, garam masala, coriander and salt. Add the tomatoes and mix well.

Cook for 5 minutes or until the mixture is slightly reduced, stirring occasionally. Fold in the cheese. Stir in the half-and-half and milk. Bring to a boil and boil for 3 to 5 minutes or until heated through, stirring constantly. Discard the bay leaves and serve immediately over the hot rice.

Yield: 6 to 8 servings

Photograph for this recipe on page 162.

Indian

Why are there so many spices in Indian food? There are several reasons why Indian dishes have more herbs and spices than most other cuisines. First, India's landscape varies greatly, yielding a wide selection of edible plants. For thousands of years Indian people have harvested many spices for food. Second, the climate allows many crops to grow throughout the year. Third, for many centuries the people of India have traded with nearby countries, which introduced foreign herbs and spices to Indian cuisine.

Czechoslovakian
Potato Dumplings

These are not fluffy dumplings as in chicken and dumplings. They are a sturdy potato dumpling served as a side dish to meat, and usually with a sweet sauerkraut/ caraway/honey dish as the side dish.

6 potatoes, peeled

1 egg yolk

1 1/2 teaspoons salt

1/2 cup (or more) all-purpose flour

Czechoslovakian

Boil the potatoes in a small amount of water in a saucepan until tender; drain. Rice the potatoes into a bowl using a potato ricer or mash with a potato masher. Let stand until cool. Add the egg yolk and salt and mix well.

Turn the potato mixture onto a lightly floured surface. Gradually add the flour to the potato mixture and knead until a dough forms. Shape the potato mixture into a long log and cut into ten equal slices.

Drop the dumplings into boiling water in a large saucepan. Boil gently for about 5 minutes. Drain the dumplings on paper towels.

The dumplings are fully cooked after the boiling process, but Czechoslovakians traditionally fry the dumplings in butter in a skillet until light brown on all sides.

Yield: 10 dumplings

Soda Bread

*This bread is popular throughout Ireland. Because it is quickly and easily prepared
it is often baked fresh for tea or even for breakfast.*

4 cups all-purpose flour

1 teaspoon salt

1 teaspoon baking soda

1 teaspoon sugar

2 cups buttermilk or sour milk

Irish

Sift the flour, salt, baking soda and sugar into a bowl. Scoop up handfuls and allow it to drop back into the bowl to aerate the mixture. Add enough of the buttermilk until a soft dough forms and mix well.

Working quickly as the buttermilk and baking soda are already reacting, knead the dough lightly. Too much kneading will toughen the dough and too little kneading means the dough will not rise properly.

Shape the dough into a round loaf about as thick as your fist. Arrange the loaf on a lightly floured baking sheet. Cut a cross in the top of the loaf using a floured knife.

Bake on the top rack in a preheated 450-degree oven for 30 to 45 minutes or until the loaf sounds hollow when lightly tapped on the bottom. Immediately wrap the loaf in a tea towel to prevent further hardening of the crust.

Wheat bread or brown soda bread is prepared in the same manner, but with whole wheat flour instead of all-purpose flour. Less buttermilk is also required.

Yield: 1 loaf

English Trifle

2 ounces sliced almonds

1 cup seedless raspberry jam

1 (9-inch) sponge cake,
cut into cubes

8 ounces fresh raspberries

3 egg yolks

3 tablespoons sugar

2 1/2 cups heavy whipping cream

English

Spread the almonds on a baking sheet. Toast in a preheated 300-degree oven or toaster oven for 2 to 10 minutes or until golden brown, stirring frequently. Remove to a plate to cool.

Spread some of the jam on each cake cube and arrange the cubes in a trifle dish or a large glass bowl. Sprinkle with the raspberries. Beat the egg yolks and sugar in a mixing bowl until pale yellow and smooth. Strain the yolk mixture into a heatproof bowl.

Heat 1 1/4 cups of the cream in a medium saucepan over medium heat. Stir a small amount of the hot cream into the egg yolk mixture. Add the egg yolk mixture to the hot cream, stirring constantly until blended.

Cook over low heat until the egg mixture is thick enough to coat the back of a spoon and of a custard consistency, stirring constantly. Remove from the heat and let stand until cool.

Beat the remaining 1 1/4 cups cream in a mixing bowl until soft peaks form. Spread the cooled custard over the cake cubes and top with the whipped cream. Sprinkle with the almonds. Chill, covered, for 2 hours before serving.

Yield: 8 servings

Baklava

I pound mixed nuts, chopped

I teaspoon cinnamon

I (16-ounce) package
phyllo pastry

I cup (2 sticks) butter, melted

I cup sugar

I cup water

$^1/_2$ cup honey

I teaspoon vanilla extract

I teaspoon grated lemon zest

Greek

Toss the nuts and cinnamon in a bowl. Unroll the pastry and cut the stack in half to fit in a 9×13-inch baking dish. Cover the pastry with waxed paper topped with a damp towel to prevent drying out. Keep the unused portion covered while assembling the baklava.

Place two sheets of the pastry in the bottom of a buttered 9×13-inch baking dish. Brush the top sheet generously with some of the melted butter. Sprinkle with 2 to 3 tablespoons of the nut mixture. Repeat the layers until all of the ingredients are used, ending with about six sheets of the pastry.

Using a sharp serrated knife, cut the layers all the way through into four long rows and then diagonally nine times to make three dozen diamonds. Bake in a preheated 350-degree oven for 50 minutes or until golden brown and crisp.

Bring the sugar and water to a boil in a small saucepan over medium heat. Stir in the honey, vanilla and lemon zest. Reduce the heat and simmer for 20 minutes. Remove the baklava from the oven and immediately pour the sugar syrup over the top. Let stand until cool. Store uncovered.

Yield: 3 dozen baklava

Rugelach

2 cups all-purpose flour

¹/2 cup granulated sugar

8 ounces cream cheese,
cut into cubes

1 cup (2 sticks) butter,
cut into cubes and chilled

¹/4 cup granulated sugar

Chopped nuts to taste

Confectioners' sugar to taste

Jewish

Combine the flour and ¹/2 cup granulated sugar in a bowl and mix well. Add the cream cheese and butter and mix until a dough forms.

Divide the dough into five equal portions. Shape each portion into a ball and wrap the balls individually in plastic wrap. Chill for 8 to 10 hours.

Roll the balls one at a time into very thin rounds on a well-floured surface. Cut each round into twelve wedges. Sprinkle the wedges with ¹/4 cup granulated sugar and nuts. Roll from the wide ends of the wedges to the points to form crescents. Arrange seam side down on an ungreased cookie sheet.

Bake in a preheated 350-degree oven for 18 minutes or until light brown. Cool on the cookie sheet for 2 minutes. Remove to a wire rack and dust with confectioners' sugar.

Yield: 5 dozen cookies

Pan Dulce

1 (1-pound) package light brown
sugar

4 eggs, beaten

2 cups all-purpose flour

1 cup chopped pecans

1 teaspoon vanilla extract

1/2 teaspoon salt

Mexican

Combine the brown sugar and eggs in a saucepan and mix well. Cook until the brown sugar melts, stirring frequently. Beat the mixture for 2 minutes; remove from the heat. Stir in the flour, pecans, vanilla and salt.

Spread the batter in a 10×15-inch baking sheet with sides. Bake in a preheated 400-degree oven for 12 minutes. Cool in the pan on a wire rack. Cut into squares.

Yield: 4 to 5 dozen squares

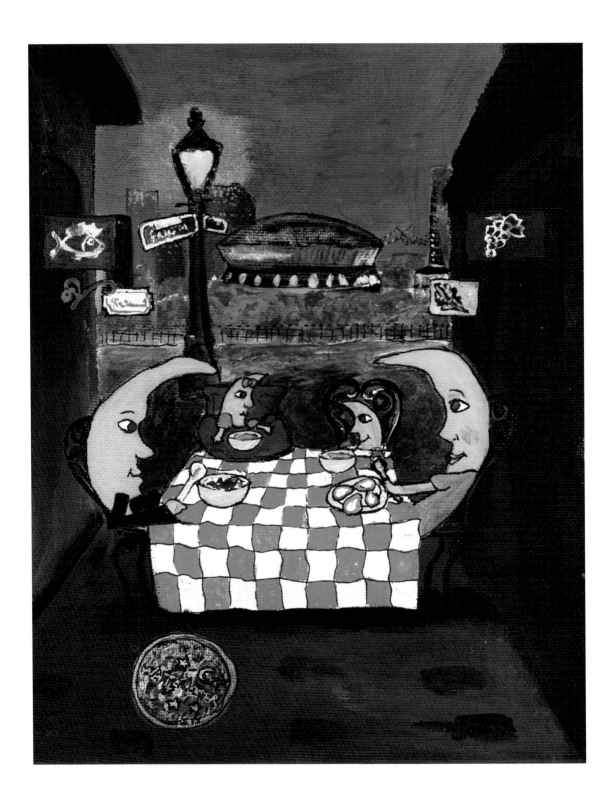

Crescent City Chefs

New Orleans is home to some of the best restaurants in the world. Luckily, though, it is possible to dine out decadently without derailing our healthy efforts.

If you're headed out with the family, many restaurants have a children's menu available. Unfortunately, the choices can be limited to fried foods and macaroni and cheese, so think beyond the kids' menu. This can present an excellent opportunity to introduce children to new and different foods, as well as encourage them to make healthy choices when away from home.

Healthy tips for eating out with kids: ask for an appetizer portion of a dinner entrée; try grilled chicken or fish instead of fried chicken fingers (ask if they can be prepared as strips that kids can pick up); encourage kids to try a new vegetable or a salad; avoid or limit sugary sodas and juice; and do not hesitate to ask if a dish can be altered to suit your taste (sauces and dressings on the side, no added oils, etc.). Resist using dessert as a reward; this only teaches children that what is on the dinner plate is not as good as dessert!

Going to a restaurant can be a fun outing for families, as well as a great time to reinforce a healthy lifestyle.

Sparkling Watermelon Soup

4^1/$_2$ cups chopped
seeded watermelon

^{1}/$_4$ cup honey

2 tablespoons lime juice

I cup unflavored or strawberry-
flavored sparkling water

I cup honeydew melon balls

I cup cantaloupe balls

I pint blueberries

Process the watermelon, honey and lime juice in a blender until puréed. Chill in the refrigerator. Combine the chilled purée and sparkling water in a large bowl and mix well.

Ladle the soup evenly into four to six soup bowls. Divide the honeydew, cantaloupe and blueberries evenly among the bowls. Garnish with 2 tablespoons chopped mint. Serve chilled.

Yield: 4 to 6 servings

April Neujean of the Samuel J. Green Charter School Edible Schoolyard
The mission of Edible Schoolyard New Orleans is to create and sustain an expansive organic garden on the public school campus of Samuel J. Green Charter School in New Orleans. It integrates organic gardening and fresh seasonal cooking into the school's curriculum, culture, and food programs. It involves students in all aspects of farming the garden—along with preparing, serving, and eating the food—as a means of awakening their senses and encouraging awareness and appreciation of the transformative values of nourishment, community, and stewardship of the land.

Organic Chicken and
Matzo Ball Soup

Soup

1 organic chicken

1/2 cup olive oil

1/4 cup sea salt

1/2 cup hard herbs, finely chopped

16 cups (1 gallon) water

1 onion, finely chopped

1 carrot, coarsely chopped

1 rib celery, finely chopped

4 bay leaves

1 bunch leeks, chopped

1 carrot, coarsely chopped

1 rib celery, finely chopped

1/4 cup vegetable oil

Matzo Balls and Assembly

1 cup matzo meal

4 organic eggs, lightly beaten

1/2 cup chicken schmaltz
(rendered fat)

12 cherry tomatoes

Kosher salt and pepper to taste

For the soup, rub the chicken with the olive oil and sprinkle with the sea salt and herbs. Arrange in a baking pan. Roast in a preheated 350-degree oven for 45 minutes; cool slightly. Pull the meat off the bones and place in a bowl, reserving the bones. Combine the reserved chicken bones, water, onion, one carrot, one rib celery and the bay leaves in a stockpot. Simmer over medium heat for 1 1/2 hours. Strain, discarding the solids and reserving the stock. Lightly sweat the leeks, one carrot and one rib celery in the vegetable oil in a stockpot for 5 minutes. Add the reserved stock and chicken and bring to a simmer. Simmer for 30 minutes.

For the matzo balls, combine the matzo meal, eggs and schmaltz in a bowl and mix well. Let rest for 15 minutes. Shape the matzo meal mixture into golf ball-size balls with oiled hands. Add the matzo balls gradually to the simmering soup. Reduce the heat and cook, covered, for 20 minutes.

Remove the soup from the heat and then remove the cover. Let rest for 10 minutes and turn each matzo ball once. Add the tomatoes and any additional herbs that may remain. Season with salt and pepper. Ladle into soup bowls.

Yield: 8 servings (1 gallon)

Jarod Tees of Lüke
When planning the menu for their brasserie, business partners Jarod Tees and John Besh incorporated dishes that they cooked at home for their own families or when they were hunting and fishing.

Turtle Soup

1 1/2 pounds turtle meat, trimmed

1/4 cup (1/2 stick) unsalted butter

8 garlic cloves, finely chopped

2 onions, finely chopped

4 ribs celery, finely chopped

2 green bell peppers, finely chopped

1 1/2 tablespoons kosher salt

1 teaspoon freshly ground pepper

2 Creole tomatoes, finely chopped

3/4 cup all-purpose flour

12 cups beef stock

1 cup Worcestershire sauce

2 tablespoons Crystal pepper sauce, or mild pepper sauce

2 tablespoons each finely chopped flat-leaf parsley and fresh thyme

5 eggs, hard-cooked and finely chopped

6 ounces fresh spinach, sliced

Zest of 3 lemons, finely chopped

1/3 cup fresh lemon juice

1/2 cup pale sherry

Kosher salt to taste

Cut the turtle meat into 1/4-inch pieces. Melt the butter in a heavy 7-quart saucepan over medium-high heat. Add the turtle meat and garlic and cook for 5 minutes or until the turtle meat is no longer pink, stirring occasionally. Stir in the onions, celery, bell peppers, 1 1/2 tablespoons salt and the pepper.

Cook for 10 minutes or just until the vegetables begin to become translucent. Stir in the tomatoes. Cook for 5 minutes, stirring frequently to prevent scorching. Reduce the heat to medium and sprinkle with the flour. Cook for 5 minutes, stirring constantly and scraping the bottom of the pan to prevent the flour from scorching. Add the stock gradually, stirring and scraping the bottom of the pan constantly to prevent lumps from forming. Stir in the Worcestershire sauce, pepper sauce, parsley and thyme. Simmer for 30 minutes.

Add the eggs, spinach, lemon zest, lemon juice and sherry and mix well. Simmer for 10 minutes. Season with salt to taste. Ladle into heated cups or soup bowls.

Yield: 16 appetizer servings, or 8 entrée servings

Chip Flanagan of Ralph's on the Park
Ralph's on the Park is located across from the entrance to beautiful City Park, which houses the world's largest collection of mature live oak trees. Turtle soup celebrates the abundant supply of reptiles in Louisiana's vast natural waterways.

Bourbon House
Butternut Squash Bisque

3 butternut squash, chopped

3 white onions, chopped

2 gallons water

1 cup packed brown sugar

2 teaspoons nutmeg

1 cup heavy cream

Salt and pepper to taste

Sweat the squash and onions in a heavy stockpot until the onions are tender. Add the water and bring to a simmer. Simmer for about 1 hour.

Process the squash mixture in batches in a food processor until smooth. Return the purée to the stockpot and stir in the brown sugar and nutmeg.

Cook for 15 minutes, stirring occasionally. Add the cream, salt and pepper and simmer just until heated through.

Strain through a fine chinois or cheesecloth. Ladle into soup bowls and garnish with crème fraîche.

Yield: 1 gallon

Darin Nesbit of Bourbon House
Founded in 2003, Dickie Brennan's Bourbon House is all about local, seasonal, fresh seafood. If it's not in season, you won't find it on the menu. Guests enjoy authentic New Orleans dishes in a lively atmosphere with huge picture windows overlooking Bourbon Street.

Oyster Chowder

1 cup (sliced crosswise into thin strips) Nueske's applewood-smoked bacon

4 cups finely chopped yellow onions

2 cups finely chopped celery

2 bay leaves

2 tablespoons salt

2 teaspoons finely chopped fresh thyme

2 teaspoons minced fresh garlic

1/2 teaspoon cayenne pepper

1/4 teaspoon white pepper

3 cups (1/4-inch pieces) peeled Idaho white potatoes

4 cups oyster liquor

1/4 cup (1/2 stick) unsalted butter

1/4 cup all-purpose flour

5 cups half-and-half

Heat a heavy saucepan over medium heat. Cook the bacon in the saucepan until crisp, stirring occasionally. Drain, reserving 2 to 3 tablespoons of the bacon drippings with the bacon in the saucepan.

Add the onions, celery and bay leaves to the saucepan and cook until the onions are tender, stirring occasionally. Stir in the salt, thyme, garlic, cayenne pepper and white pepper. Cook for 1 minute, stirring constantly. Add the potatoes and liquor and bring to a boil.

Melt 1/4 cup butter in a small skillet over low heat. Whisk in the flour until blended. Cook for 1 minute, whisking constantly. Stir the roux into the boiling chowder mixture.

Reduce the heat to low and simmer for 5 minutes, whisking occasionally. Add the half-and-half and whisk until blended. Bring to a boil. Reduce the heat to low and simmer for 10 minutes. Discard the bay leaves.

2 tablespoons unsalted butter

3/4 cup thinly sliced green onions

1/2 cup finely chopped
flat-leaf parsley

60 freshly shucked
Louisiana oysters

Melt 2 tablespoons butter in a large skillet over medium-high heat. Add the green onions and parsley and cook for 5 to 10 seconds. Add the oysters and cook just until the oysters curl. Do not overcook the oysters.

Ladle the chowder into soup bowls and add six oysters and some of the green onion mixture to each bowl. Serve immediately.

This recipe uses oyster liquor, or oyster water, which is a key ingredient in most oyster soups. This product is available from most oyster suppliers. If unavailable, make your own. Place fresh oysters in a mixing bowl and pour in 5 cups ice-cold water. Stir and then strain. This should produce the 4 cups of oyster liquor required for this recipe.

Yield: 10 servings

Frank Brigtsen of Brigtsen's Restaurant
Frank Brigtsen, owner of Brigtsen's Restaurant, utilizes his native New Orleans palate to create dishes that pay tribute to the traditions of Louisiana cuisine. He has applied an inventive personal touch to seven years of training in classic Louisiana cooking under internationally acclaimed Chef Paul Prudhomme. Patrons praise his ability to ingeniously incorporate local ingredients into his unique menu, which changes daily.

Lasagna

1 pound ground beef

1 (16-ounce) can tomatoes

1 (12-ounce) can tomato paste

1 tablespoon crushed dried basil

1 1/2 teaspoons salt

1 garlic clove, minced

10 ounces lasagna noodles

3 cups ricotta cheese or cottage cheese

1/2 cup (2 ounces) grated Parmesan cheese

2 tablespoons parsley flakes

2 eggs, beaten

1 teaspoon salt

1/2 teaspoon pepper

16 ounces mozzarella cheese, shredded

Brown the ground meat in a saucepan, stirring until crumbly; drain. Stir in the tomatoes, tomato paste, basil, 1 1/2 teaspoons salt and the garlic. Simmer for 30 minutes, stirring occasionally.

Cook the pasta using the package directions. Drain and rinse. Combine the ricotta cheese, Parmesan cheese, parsley flakes, eggs, 1 teaspoon salt and the pepper in a bowl and mix well.

Layer the pasta, ricotta cheese mixture, mozzarella cheese and meat sauce one-half at a time in the order listed in a 9×13-inch baking dish. Bake in a preheated 375-degree oven for 30 minutes. Let stand for 10 minutes before serving.

Yield: 6 to 8 servings

Sean Payton, Head Coach New Orleans Saints
Sean Payton, head coach of the New Orleans Saints, ranks among the most successful head coaches in franchise history. He is the only coach to lead the Saints to an NFC Championship and was a unanimous choice for NFL Coach of the Year. He has been the architect of an offense that has rewritten the club's record books, and since his arrival he has instilled a winning culture within the organization.

Marvelous Miniature Meat Loaves

1 pound ground beef

1 (6-ounce) package stove-top stuffing mix

1 cup water

1 teaspoon garlic powder

Barbecue sauce to taste

Shredded Colby Jack cheese or cheese of choice to taste

Combine the ground beef, stuffing mix and water in a bowl and mix well. Mix in the garlic powder. Press the ground beef mixture evenly into twelve medium muffin cups sprayed with nonstick cooking spray.

Make an indentation in the center of each with the back of a spoon. Pour the desired amount of barbecue sauce into each indentation.

Bake in a preheated 375-degree oven for 30 minutes or until the meat loaves are cooked through. Sprinkle with cheese and bake for 5 minutes longer or until the cheese melts. Let stand for 10 minutes before serving.

Yield: 1 dozen miniature meat loaves

Ryan Bowen of the New Orleans Hornets
This is an easy recipe and one that kids really enjoy. Our kids like helping us make this recipe. It can also be made in advance and frozen, which is helpful for busy moms.

Cajun-Style Chicken Breast with
Chili Bean Maque Choux

A simple smear of Creole mustard, which gets added heat from horseradish, and a little extra seasoning give a chicken breast new sass. Here the chicken is paired with a speedy version of maque choux, a Louisiana sauté of beans and corn. You'd be hard-pressed to find a simpler, more satisfying weekday supper. For this dish, the chicken breasts can be broiled, grilled, or pan-seared.

Maque Choux

2 ears sweet white or yellow corn, or 1 1/2 cups thawed frozen corn kernels

1 tablespoon olive oil or vegetable oil

1 tablespoon butter

1/2 yellow onion, chopped

1 jalapeño chile, seeded and minced

1 garlic clove, minced

1 (14-ounce) can red beans, kidney beans or chili beans, drained

1/2 cup chopped seeded peeled fresh tomato or undrained canned tomato

1/4 cup water

Salt to taste

Hot red pepper sauce to taste

1 tablespoon butter

For the maque choux, shuck the corn and remove the silk. Cut the corn kernels from the cob into a bowl, being careful not to cut too close to the cob where the kernels are dry and starchy. Heat the olive oil and 1 tablespoon butter in a skillet until foamy; add the onion. Cook for 2 to 3 minutes. Stir in the corn kernels, jalapeño chile and garlic.

Cook for about 3 minutes and then stir in the beans, tomato and water. Season with salt and hot sauce. Cook until heated through; swirl in 1 tablespoon butter. Remove from the heat and cover to keep warm.

Susan Spicer of Bayona
Nested in a two hundred-year-old Creole Cottage in the oldest section of the historic French Quarter, Bayona is one of the jewels in the "Big Easy" culinary crown. Founded in 1990, the restaurant was named for Dauphine Street's Spanish name, Camino de Bayona. Susan Spicer is a one-woman industry in New Orleans. She was named one of Food and Wine's *ten Best New Chefs and received the James Beard Award for Best Chef, Southeast Region in 1993. Bayona was featured in the 1994* Bon Appétit *and in* Food and Wine's *Thanksgiving issue in 2000.*

Chicken and Assembly

2 tablespoons olive oil or
vegetable oil

2 tablespoons Creole mustard or
whole grain mustard

1 teaspoon salt

1/2 teaspoon black pepper

1/2 teaspoon cayenne pepper

4 (6-ounce) boneless skinless
chicken breasts

1 to 2 tablespoons vegetable oil

2 tablespoon chopped scallions

For the chicken, mix the olive oil, Creole mustard, salt, black pepper and cayenne pepper in a small bowl. Coat the chicken evenly with the mustard mixture. Marinate, covered, in the refrigerator for 15 minutes to several hours.

Heat the vegetable oil in a large nonstick skillet over medium-high heat. Pat any excess marinade from the chicken using a paper towel and add the chicken to the hot oil.

Sear for 3 to 4 minutes per side or until the chicken is brown and cooked through. Or you can grill the chicken over hot coals or broil it.

Spoon equal portions of the maque choux onto each of four serving plates and top each serving with one chicken breast.

The corn and beans together provide a good amount of starch, so this dish needs nothing more than a tossed salad or a simple green vegetable. Of course, a big slice of warm corn bread would be delicious, too.

Yield: 4 servings

Blackened Redfish Burgers

6 (8-ounce) redfish fillets, chilled

6 tablespoons canola oil

2 tablespoons olive oil

$1/2$ cup thinly sliced green onions

2 tablespoons Creole seasoning

Chill all the nonelectric parts of a grinder, including the plate with $3/16$-inch holes, in the freezer for about 5 minutes. Chill a large mixing bowl in the freezer.

Grind the fish using the chilled grinder fitted with the $3/16$-inch plate and place the ground fish in the chilled bowl. Chill the ground fish if not cold to the touch. Or, finely chop the fish by hand and chill for about 35 to 45 minutes or until cold.

Add 6 tablespoons canola oil, the olive oil, green onions and Creole seasoning to the chilled fish and mix until the fish is coated with the oils and the remaining ingredients are evenly distributed.

Shape 1 to 2 teaspoons of the fish mixture into a small sample patty. This sample patty will be cooked after all of the remaining patties have been chilled in order to determine if the patties need to be seasoned with salt and pepper.

Shape the remaining fish mixture into six patties approximately $3/4$ inch thick and $41/4$ inches in diameter. Arrange the large patties and sample patty on a platter and chill, covered, for 1 to 3 hours.

Canola oil for coating

Kosher salt and freshly ground
pepper to taste

Lettuce leaves

Sliced tomatoes

Thinly sliced red onion

6 sesame seed hamburger buns,
toasted and buttered

Coat a 13-inch cast-iron skillet with canola oil and heat over high heat for 2 minutes or until hot. Add the sample patty to the hot skillet and blacken to taste. Taste the sample patty and determine if salt and pepper are needed. If needed, sprinkle the six large patties with salt and pepper.

Blacken the patties three at a time in the hot skillet for about 4 minutes per side or until dark brown. To test for doneness, transfer one of the patties to a plate and insert the tip of a thin-bladed knife into the thickest portion of the patty for about 10 seconds. Remove the knife and lay the tip of the blade flat against the inside of your wrist. If the tip feels hot against the skin, the patties are done.

To serve open-faced, arrange lettuce, tomato and onion on the bottom halves of the buns and the fish patties on the top halves of the buns on serving plates.

Yield: 6 burgers

Gregg Collier of Red Fish Grill
Red Fish Grill is a Ralph Brennan–owned casual New Orleans seafood restaurant at the foot of Bourbon and Canal Streets. The hand-painted tables and sea of metal fish in neon swimming overhead have played host to many a New Orleans family celebration. Blackened Redfish Burgers, also featured in Ralph Brennan's New Orleans Seafood Cookbook, *are healthier alternatives to traditional beef burgers.*

Slow-Cooked Louisiana Shrimp
and Andouille over Grits

Shrimp Stock

1 pound shrimp shells

1/4 cup canola oil

1 onion, coarsely chopped

1 rib celery, coarsely chopped

1 carrot, peeled and
coarsely chopped

1 leek bulb, chopped

4 garlic cloves, crushed

3 quarts water

1 bay leaf

1 sprig of thyme

Cheesy Grits

4 cups water

1 teaspoon salt

1 cup McEwens stone-ground
organic white grits

1/2 cup mascarpone cheese

2 tablespoons butter

For the stock, toast the shells in the canola oil in a stockpot over high heat for 10 minutes, stirring frequently. Add the onion, celery, carrot, leek and garlic and sweat the vegetables for 3 minutes. Stir in the water, bay leaf and thyme and bring to a boil.

Reduce the heat to medium-low and cook until the stock is reduced by half. Strain the stock, discarding the solids. Any unused stock may be stored, covered, in the refrigerator or freezer for future use.

For the grits, bring the water and salt to a boil in a saucepan and add the grits, stirring constantly. Reduce the heat to low.

Simmer for about 20 minutes, stirring constantly to prevent the grits from sticking to the bottom of the pan. Add the cheese and butter and stir until blended. Remove from the heat and cover to keep warm.

John Besh of Restaurant August, Besh Steak, Lüke, and La Provence
"Sundays are the days that I get to spend with my family. With four young sons, I am always looking for ways to involve them in cooking. This recipe for Shrimp and Grits is great for that. There are steps that my twelve-year-old, Brendan, is now confident enough to manage, as well as simple tasks that four-year-old Andrew can do. Afterward, we enjoy eating it as a family around the table, sharing stories of our day."

Shrimp, Andouille and Assembly

30 jumbo Louisiana shrimp, peeled and deveined

Salt and pepper to taste

Creole spices to taste

2 tablespoons olive oil

6 tablespoons finely chopped andouille

2 tablespoons finely chopped piquillo chiles

1 tablespoon minced garlic

1 tablespoon minced shallot

1 tablespoon chopped thyme

2 tablespoons butter

2 cups chopped tomatoes

1 tablespoon chopped chives

1 teaspoon fresh lemon juice

1/2 cup fresh chervil

For the shrimp and andouille, season the shrimp with salt, pepper and Creole spices. Heat a large saucepan over medium heat. Pour the olive oil into the saucepan.

Sauté the shrimp in the hot oil until the shrimp begin to brown and are partially cooked. Remove the shrimp to a bowl using a slotted spoon, reserving the pan drippings. Add the sausage, piquillo chiles, garlic, shallot and thyme to the reserved pan drippings and mix well.

Sauté until the mixture is fragrant. Stir in 4 cups of the stock and bring to a low simmer. Add the butter and cook until thickened. Return the shrimp to the saucepan and cook until the shrimp are cooked through. Stir in the tomatoes, chives and lemon juice.

Spoon four heaping tablespoons of the grits into the center of each of four large bowls. Arrange five of the shrimp, with tails facing in, in each serving of grits. Spoon the andouille sauce around the grits and sprinkle with the chervil.

Yield: 6 servings

Shrimp Felicia

4 jumbo shrimp, peeled
and deveined

1 teaspoon lemon juice

Salt and black pepper to taste

3 tablespoons olive oil

1 1/2 tablespoons minced onion

1 1/2 tablespoons minced garlic

1/2 cup chopped tomato

2 tablespoons Pernod

Pinch of fennel pollen

1/4 teaspoon red pepper flakes

Hot cooked linguini or
angel hair pasta

Butterfly the shrimp scampi-style. Drizzle with the lemon juice and sprinkle with salt and black pepper.

Heat the olive oil in a skillet over medium heat and add the onion and garlic. Sauté for several minutes and then stir in the tomato. Add the shrimp and toss two or three times. Add the liqueur, fennel pollen and red pepper flakes and mix well.

Cook for several minutes or until the liquid is slightly reduced and the shrimp are cooked through. Add pasta and cook over low heat for 1 minute.

Serve in a pasta bowl with the shrimp on top. Garnish with parsley tucked under a lemon wedge.

Yield: 1 serving

Vincent Pigna of Gelato Pazzo Caffè
"We are a family-owned and operated Caffè like you find in Italy, where we prepare not only incredible and rich-tasting homemade artisan gelato, but strive to offer a true Italian Caffè experience." This recipe is named after my wife, Felicia, who likes shrimp.

Calas

6 tablespoons all-purpose flour

3 tablespoons (heaping) sugar

2 teaspoons baking powder

$^1/_4$ teaspoon salt

Dash of nutmeg

2 cups cooked rice

2 eggs, lightly beaten

$^1/_4$ teaspoon vanilla extract

Vegetable oil

Confectioners' sugar to taste

Whisk the flour, sugar, baking powder, salt and nutmeg in a bowl until combined. Stir in the rice. Add the eggs and vanilla and mix well.

Heat enough oil for deep-frying in a skillet to 360 degrees. Drop the rice mixture by spoonfuls into the hot oil and fry until brown on all sides. Remove from the oil using a slotted spoon; drain on paper towels. Sprinkle with confectioners' sugar and serve hot.

Yield: 12 calas

Poppy Tooker, Local Food Hero
Recognized by the Times Picayune *as a "Hero of the Storm," Poppy's wide-ranging restoration efforts included Dooky Chase Restaurant, Gendusa Bakery, and Angelo Brocato's Ice Cream and Confectionery. Inspired by Poppy's far-reaching restoration and improvement efforts, The International Association of Culinary Professionals recognized her at their 2008 conference with their first-ever Community Service Award.*

Easy Chocolate Truffles

1 cup heavy cream

2 cups (12 ounces) semisweet chocolate chips

2 tablespoons butter, softened

1 teaspoon vanilla extract

2 cups confectioners' sugar or baking cocoa

Bring the cream to a boil in a small saucepan. Remove from the heat and stir in the chocolate chips with a wooden spoon until blended. Return the mixture to the heat to completely melt the chocolate if needed. Add the butter and vanilla and stir until incorporated.

Pour the chocolate mixture into a shallow dish and chill, covered with plastic wrap, for 1 hour. Shape the chocolate mixture by teaspoonfuls into 1/2-inch balls.

Roll the truffles in the confectioners' sugar until completely coated. Store in an airtight container in the refrigerator.

Yield: 2 dozen truffles

Joel Dondis and Tariq Hanna of Sucré
Since launching his first entrepreneurial venture in 1993, Joel has become a key player on the New Orleans hospitality and restaurant scene. Joel Catering and Event Planning is widely regarded to be a local and national industry leader and the largest off-premises catering and event planning company in New Orleans. Together Tariq and Joel have created Sucré to be a pastry experience unlike any the city has ever seen.

The Perfect Cookie

These cookies are perfect for an afternoon snack, pre-sports fueling, tailgating parties, or any gathering.

1 cup whole wheat flour

1 teaspoon baking soda

1 teaspoon cinnamon

1/2 teaspoon salt (optional)

3/4 cup Brummel and Brown
butter-style spread

1 1/2 cups granulated fructose

3/4 cup ground flax seeds

2 eggs

1 teaspoon vanilla extract

3 cups rolled oats

Whisk the whole wheat flour, baking soda, cinnamon and salt in a bowl. Beat the butter-style spread and fructose in a mixing bowl until creamy. Add the flax seeds and beat until combined. Add the eggs and vanilla and beat until incorporated. Mix in the flour mixture; stir in the oats.

Drop the dough by rounded tablespoonfuls onto an ungreased cookie sheet. Bake in a preheated 350-degree oven for 8 to 10 minutes for chewy cookies or 10 to 12 minutes for crisp cookies. Cool on the cookie sheet for 1 minute. Remove to a wire rack to cool completely. Store in an airtight container.

Only low-glycemic ingredients that will not spike blood sugar and insulin levels are used in preparing these cookies. They contain flax seeds, which are rich in Omega-3 fatty acids. The cookie ingredients are 100 percent natural with no refined flours, sugars, or artificial fat or sugar substitutes.

Yield: 4 dozen cookies

**Molly Kimball of Ochsner's
Elmwood Fitness Center**
Molly is a Sports and Lifestyle Dietitian and is Board Certified as a Specialist in Sports Dietetics. She manages the nutrition program at Elmwood. Additionally, Molly is a weekly columnist for the Times-Picayune *newspaper. "Eating healthfully does not have to be all-or-nothing. Teaching children how to fit their favorite foods into a mostly nutritious diet will give them the tools they need to stay healthy for life."*

Mr. Ralph's
Ice Cream Sandwiches

1 cup all-purpose flour

1/2 cup plus 2 tablespoons baking cocoa

1 teaspoon baking powder

1/2 teaspoon baking soda

1/2 teaspoon salt

1 1/4 cups sugar

1/3 cup vegetable oil

2 eggs

1/2 cup warm water

Coat the bottom and sides of an 11×17-inch jellyroll pan with nonstick cooking spray. Line the bottom of the pan with baking parchment and spray the baking parchment with nonstick cooking spray.

Whisk the flour, baking cocoa, baking powder, baking soda and salt in a bowl. Whisk the sugar and oil in a bowl until the mixture resembles wet sand. Add the eggs one at a time, whisking constantly until combined after each addition. Add one-third of the dry ingredients and whisk until incorporated. Whisk in half the warm water and then half of the remaining dry ingredients. Whisk in the remaining warm water and then the remaining dry ingredients until blended.

Spread the batter in the prepared pan using an icing spatula or rubber spatula. The batter will be fairly thin. Tap the pan on the countertop about three times to expel any air bubbles. Bake in a preheated 375-degree oven for 14 to 16 minutes or until the cake bounces back when lightly pressed. Cool in the pan on a wire rack for about 25 minutes or until completely cooled.

Run a sharp knife around the edges of the cake to loosen. Place a piece of baking parchment cut to the size of the cake over the cake and then place a large cutting board or the bottom of a baking sheet on top of the baking parchment. Invert the whole assembly and tap the underside of the pan to make sure the cake releases. Lift the jellyroll pan off the cake and discard the baking parchment from the bottom of the cake. Trim a thin strip from the sides of the cake and square the corners to make the cake look neat and free of any dry edges. Cut the cake crosswise into two equal rectangles.

2 pints chocolate malt ice cream
or flavor of choice

Caramel ice cream topping
(optional)

Hot fudge ice cream topping
(optional)

Coat the bottom and sides of an 11×17-inch jellyroll pan Line a small baking sheet with baking parchment. The baking sheet should be only slightly larger than the cake rectangles. Carefully transfer one of the cake rectangles to the prepared baking sheet. Let the ice cream stand at room temperature for 15 minutes or until slightly softened. Spread the softened ice cream over the cake rectangle and top with the remaining cake rectangle. Freeze, uncovered, for 3 to 10 hours or until the ice cream hardens. If prepared more than 1 day in advance, allow the ice cream to harden and then cover loosely with foil. Store in the freezer.

Slice the frozen cake lengthwise into halves and then cut each half crosswise into thirds. Spoon 1 to 2 tablespoons of the caramel topping onto each of six chilled dessert plates and arrange one ice cream sandwich on each plate. Drizzle 1 tablespoon or more of the hot fudge topping over each sandwich. Serve immediately. Or, wrap each sandwich individually in plastic wrap and then place in a sealable plastic bag. Freeze for future use.

Yield: 6 ice cream sandwiches

Chris Montero of BACCO
BACCO is Ralph Brennan's Creole Italian eatery in the heart of the New Orleans French Quarter. This dish was created to honor Ralph's love of ice cream. For a healthier snack, substitute low-fat or no-added-sugar ice cream.

Crescent City Conditional Cooking

Kids may have specific dietary needs or restrictions, and it is important for parents to teach them how to adapt to these issues. Certain health conditions require specific dietary restrictions, including diabetes, gluten intolerance, and food allergies, to name a few. Other situations, such as religious beliefs, may also affect the way we cook, and recipes may be altered accordingly. There are numerous resources available to show parents how to accommodate special dietary requirements so that children will be able to adapt when with their peers. Explore different ways to include kids' favorite foods so they will still be able to enjoy a varied diet along with their friends.

Healthy Snack Granola Bars

1 cup (2 sticks) margarine

3/4 cup packed brown sugar

1/2 cup granulated sugar

2 tablespoons grade-A
maple syrup

4 cups rolled oats

1 cup shredded coconut

1/3 cup chopped pecans

1 cup dried apricots or dried fruit
of choice, chopped

Dairy-Free
Nutritional Profiles 230–233

Combine the margarine, brown sugar, granulated sugar and syrup in a large saucepan. Cook until blended, stirring occasionally. Stir in the oats, coconut, pecans and apricots.

Spread the batter in a greased 9×12-inch baking sheet with sides, pressing down to make sure the surface is smooth. Bake in a preheated 325-degree oven for 30 minutes.

Cool in the pan on a wire rack for 20 minutes. Cut into bars. Store in an airtight container.

Yield: 12 servings

Basil Zucchini Soup

Vegetarians love this soup. It has a beautiful color and is perfect as a tasty first course in the summer or any warm month in New Orleans.

2 tablespoons olive oil

1/2 cup chopped onion

12 ounces zucchini, chopped

Salt and pepper to taste

1 1/2 cups water

1 cup vegetable broth

2 cups packed fresh basil

2 teaspoons minced garlic

1 teaspoon red wine vinegar

Heat the olive oil in a saucepan until hot and add the onion. Sauté until the onion is tender. Stir in the zucchini, salt and pepper. Sauté for 4 minutes. Add the water and broth and mix well.

Simmer, covered, for 10 minutes. Stir in the basil and garlic. Simmer for 1 minute. Remove from the heat and let stand until cool.

Process the zucchini mixture in a food processor or blender until puréed. Mix in the vinegar. Serve chilled or at room temperature.

Yield: 6 (1/2-cup) servings

Vegetarian
Nutritional Profiles 230–233

Keep in mind that living a healthy lifestyle includes eating right, exercising, and getting plenty of rest. It all pays off when you take care of yourself. **A benefit of healthy living described by a Crescent City Cutie:** *"Staying healthy will help you grow bigger so you can be tall enough to ride the roller coaster."*
—Noah Bregman

Olivia's Feel-Good Chicken Soup

This recipe was created for children using their favorite ingredients—rice, carrots, and chicken—the perfect comfort food!

4 cups fat-free chicken broth

4 to 6 cups water

16 ounces baby carrots, chopped

1 cup chopped celery

1 cup short grain brown rice

1/2 cup wild rice

1/2 cup fresh parsley, chopped

2 Knorr chicken bouillon cubes

1 tablespoon freshly ground pepper

1 1/2 pounds boneless skinless chicken breasts or tenders

Salt and pepper to taste

Combine the broth, 4 cups water, the carrots, celery, brown rice, wild rice, parsley, bouillon cubes and 1 tablespoon pepper in a stockpot. Bring to a simmer over medium heat and simmer for 1 hour, stirring occasionally.

Season the chicken with salt and pepper to taste. Arrange the chicken in a single layer on a baking sheet. Bake in a preheated 400-degree oven for 25 minutes. The chicken should be cooked through but still moist. Cool slightly and cut the chicken into bite-size pieces.

Immediately stir the chicken into the soup mixture. Add the remaining 2 cups water as needed for the desired consistency as the soup simmers and the rice expands. Season with salt and ladle into soup bowls.

Yield: 10 (1-cup) servings

Photograph for this recipe on page 210.

When You're Sick
Nutritional Profiles 230–233

Chicken Stock

4 pounds chicken carcasses,
including necks and backs

1 large onion, cut into quarters

12 baby carrots

4 ribs celery, cut into halves

1 leek bulb, cut lengthwise
into halves

10 sprigs of thyme

10 sprigs of parsley with stems

2 bay leaves

4 sage leaves

8 to 10 peppercorns

2 garlic cloves, minced

2 gallons cold water

When You're Sick
Nutritional Profiles 230–233

Combine the chicken carcasses, onion, carrots, celery, leek, thyme, parsley, bay leaves, sage leaves, peppercorns and garlic in a 12-quart stockpot. Place an opened steamer basket directly over the ingredients and pour in the cold water.

Cook over high heat until bubbles begin to appear. Reduce the heat to medium-low to maintain a low gentle simmer.

Simmer for 6 to 8 hours, skimming the foam from the stock every 15 to 20 minutes. Add hot water as needed to keep the bones and vegetables submerged.

Strain the stock into a large heatproof bowl, discarding the solids. Immediately place the bowl in a container of ice or ice water and let stand until a thermometer registers 40 degrees or below.

Chill, covered, for 8 to 10 hours. Skim off any solidified fat from the surface. Store, covered, in the refrigerator for 2 to 3 days or freeze for up to 3 months. Boil the required amount of stock for 2 minutes before using in your favorite recipes. Use as a base for soups and sauces.

Yield: 24 servings

Orange Jell-O Salad

1 (3-ounce) package orange Jell-O

1 cup boiling water

1 (11-ounce) can mandarin oranges, drained

1 (6-ounce) can crushed pineapple, drained

1 cup miniature marshmallows

1/2 cup chopped pecans (optional)

12 ounces Cool Whip whipped topping

Dissolve the Jell-O in the boiling water in a large heatproof bowl. Let stand until cool.

Stir in the mandarin oranges, pineapple, marshmallows and pecans. Fold in the whipped topping. Chill, covered, for 8 to 10 hours or until set.

Yield: 12 (1-cup) servings

When You're Sick
Nutritional Profiles 230–233

In addition to teaching children the benefits of healthy living, be sure to discuss the consequences of poor eating habits and lack of exercise. Childhood obesity, diseases, lack of energy, and poor concentration can inhibit students' abilities in school and affect every aspect of their lives. **A Crescent City Cutie explains why healthful snacks should replace sugary ones:** *"...because you do not want to get a cavity in your tooth."*
—Mary Kate Luetkemeier

Grilled Asian Steak Salad

Asian Dressing

2 tablespoons light soy sauce

2 tablespoons fresh lemon juice

1 tablespoon granulated Splenda

2 teaspoons minced garlic

2 teaspoons sesame oil

2 teaspoons white wine vinegar

1 teaspoon extra-virgin olive oil

1/2 teaspoon minced fresh ginger

1/4 teaspoon crushed red pepper

1/4 teaspoon Tabasco sauce

Salad

7 cups chopped romaine

1 1/2 cups grape tomatoes, cut into halves

1 1/2 cup baby carrots, sliced

3/4 cup snow peas, cut into thirds

1/2 red bell pepper, thinly sliced

1/2 yellow bell pepper, thinly sliced

8 ounces flank steak, trimmed, grilled and chilled

For the dressing, whisk the soy sauce, lemon juice, Splenda, garlic, sesame oil, vinegar, olive oil, ginger, red pepper and Tabasco sauce in a bowl until combined.

For the salad, toss the romaine, tomatoes, carrots, snow peas and bell peppers in a salad bowl.

Slice the flank steak as desired and add to the salad. Add the dressing and toss to coat. Serve chilled.

Yield: 6 servings

Diabetic
Nutritional Profiles 230–233

Tuna and Veggie Salad

2/3 cup chopped radishes

2/3 cup chopped celery

2/3 cup chopped carrots

1 (6-ounce) can water-pack tuna, drained

2 tablespoons red wine vinegar

1 teaspoon Italian herbs or any salt-free seasoning

2 teaspoons granulated Splenda

2 tablespoons olive oil

Low-Carb
Nutritional Profiles 230–233

Combine the radishes, celery, carrots and tuna in a bowl and mix well. Whisk the vinegar and Italian herbs in a measuring cup until combined. Stir in the Splenda. Add the olive oil and whisk until the oil is emulsified.

Add the dressing to the tuna mixture and mix well. Serve immediately or chill, covered, in the refrigerator.

Yield: 2 servings

Explore the different ways that simple foods such as fruits and vegetables can be cooked. Eating these raw is always an option, but don't forget that you can bake, steam, fry, or sauté them, too. Adding variety not only to the foods you eat but the way that you cook them helps keep meals from being mundane. **A cooking suggestion by a Crescent City Cutie:** *"...broccoli. Put it in a steaming bag."*
—Samantha Knister

Beef Tzimmes

1 (10-pound) beef brisket or bottom round roast

Seasonings of choice to taste

1 cup peeled baby carrots

3/4 cup (1-inch) slices sweet potato

1 pound mixed dried fruit (apricots, prunes and peaches)

1/2 cup honey or packed brown sugar

1 large onion, chopped

1 teaspoon salt

2 tablespoons shortening or chicken fat

2 tablespoons all-purpose flour

Kosher
Nutritional Profiles 230–233

Season the brisket with seasonings of choice. Sear on all sides in a Dutch oven or heavy saucepan. Add the carrots, sweet potato, dried fruit, honey, onion, salt and enough water to cover. Bring to a boil and skim any foam from the surface. Reduce the heat.

Simmer for 2 1/2 to 3 hours or until the brisket is fork-tender, adding additional water as needed. Taste and adjust the seasonings.

Make a roux with the shortening and flour and stir into the brisket mixture. Place the brisket mixture in a large baking dish.

Bake in a preheated 350-degree oven for 30 minutes or until the beef and vegetables are brown. You may prepare in advance and store, covered, in the refrigerator. Bake just before serving.

Yield: 10 servings

Wheatballs and
Spaghetti Squash

A take on the traditional meatballs and spaghetti, this dish is low in fat, low in refined carbohydrates, high in fiber, and does not taste like you're "being good."

4 slices turkey bacon

1 pound ground turkey

3 scallions, trimmed and chopped

1/2 cup (or less) wheat bran

Salt and pepper or your favorite seasonings to taste

2 tablespoons extra-virgin olive oil

1 (24-ounce) jar pasta sauce

1 (2-pound) spaghetti squash

1/2 cup (2 ounces) freshly grated Romano cheese

Low-Fat, Low-Carb, High Fiber
Nutritional Profiles 230–233

Arrange the bacon in a microwave-safe dish. Microwave until crisp; drain. Or, bake in the oven until crisp. Crumble the bacon over the ground turkey in a bowl. Add the scallions, wheat bran, salt and pepper and mix gently. Shape into twelve to sixteen small wheatballs.

Heat the olive oil in a large skillet over medium-high heat. Panfry the wheatballs in the hot oil for 5 minutes or until light brown on all sides; do not fry longer than 5 minutes. Mix in the pasta sauce. Cook over medium heat for 15 to 20 minutes, stirring occasionally.

Cut the squash lengthwise into halves and prick with a fork several times. Arrange the halves cut side down in a microwave-safe dish. Microwave for about 15 minutes or until the squash can be easily shredded with a fork.

Shred the squash evenly among four serving plates. Top each serving with three or four wheatballs and an equal portion of the sauce. Sprinkle with the cheese.

You may substitute ground or whole flax seeds, cooked brown rice or wild rice, or even leftover couscous for the wheat bran.

Yield: 4 servings

Baked Flounder in Dill Sauce

1 (8-ounce) flounder fillet

1/2 teaspoon salt

1 tablespoon light mayonnaise

1 tablespoon light soy sauce

2 tablespoons chopped fresh
dill weed, or 1 tablespoon
dried dill weed

2 teaspoons honey mustard or
whole-grain mustard

2 garlic cloves, pressed

Diabetic
Nutritional Profiles 230–233

Cut the fillet into 2-inch slices and sprinkle with the salt. Arrange in a baking dish. Combine the mayonnaise, soy sauce, dill weed, mustard and garlic in a bowl and mix well.

Spoon the mayonnaise mixture over the flounder. Marinate, covered, in the refrigerator for several hours, turning occasionally.

Bake in a preheated 375-degree oven until the flounder is opaque but still pink. White fish is a sign of overbaking.

Yield: 4 servings

Sesame Tilapia

2 (4-ounce) tilapia fillets

1/4 cup sesame oil

1 garlic clove, minced

1 teaspoon Italian seasoning

Kosher salt to taste

Freshly ground pepper to taste

Low-Carb
Nutritional Profiles 230–233

Place the tilapia in a bowl and drizzle with the sesame oil. Add the garlic, Italian seasoning, salt and pepper and turn to coat. Marinate, covered, in the refrigerator for 30 minutes or longer.

Arrange the tilapia and marinade in a baking dish. Bake in a preheated 350-degree oven for 30 minutes or until the tilapia flakes easily.

Yield: 2 servings

Use a clean spoon each time you taste your recipe as it cooks. **A healthy eating tip from a Crescent City Cutie:** *"Don't put your fingers in the food when you're cooking. That's gross!"*

—Brennan Scott

Cauliflower Soufflé

Serve for lunch, as an appetizer, or as an entrée.

1 head cauliflower, separated into florets

4 ounces fine noodles

3 tablespoons chopped parsley

6 tablespoons margarine, softened

1/4 teaspoon salt

1/2 cup mayonnaise

3 tablespoons chopped parsley

1 tablespoon finely grated onion

1 tablespoon lemon juice

Dash of cayenne pepper

2 egg whites

Vegetarian
Nutritional Profiles 230–233

Cook the cauliflower in a steamer until tender; drain. Cover to keep warm. Cook the pasta using the package directions; drain.

Toss the hot pasta with 3 tablespoons parsley in a bowl. Add the margarine and salt and mix until the margarine melts. Spoon into a baking dish and top with the cauliflower.

Combine the mayonnaise, 3 tablespoons parsley, the onion, lemon juice and cayenne pepper in a bowl and mix well. Beat the egg whites in a mixing bowl until stiff peaks form. Fold the mayonnaise mixture into the egg whites.

Spread the mayonnaise mixture over the prepared layers. Broil until the top is brown. Watch carefully as this takes only a short time.

Yield: 10 (1/2-cup) servings

Hearty Grits

6 ounces frozen chopped spinach, thawed and drained

1 1/2 cups chicken stock or chicken broth

1 cup low-fat milk

1 cup grits (do not use instant)

1/2 teaspoon salt

1/8 teaspoon garlic salt

6 ounces goat cheese, crumbled

When You're Sick
Nutritional Profiles 230–233

Press any excess moisture from the spinach. Bring the stock, milk, grits, salt and garlic salt to a boil in a medium saucepan over medium heat. Reduce the heat to low.

Simmer for 15 minutes or until the grits have absorbed most of the stock. Stir in the spinach and cheese. Cook until the cheese melts, stirring constantly.

Substitute mozzarella cheese or mild Cheddar cheese for the goat cheese when mild but hearty dishes are required.

Yield: 6 servings

Photograph for this recipe on page 210.

Be aware of expiration dates on food items when gathering your recipe ingredients. Always respect what the food label says. And when in doubt, throw it out. **A safety tip from a Crescent City Cutie:** *"Make sure the food is not poisonous!"*
—Wilson Engelhardt

Pancakes

This pancake mix is free of wheat, dairy, soy, nut, and egg.

1/2 cup sorghum flour

1/2 cup potato starch

1/4 cup garbanzo bean flour

1 to 2 tablespoons brown sugar

2 teaspoons baking powder

1/2 teaspoon salt

Sprinkle of xanthan gum or guar gum

1 cup rice milk

2 tablespoons vegetable oil

1 teaspoon vanilla extract

1/4 cup mashed banana

Mix the sorghum flour, potato starch, garbanzo bean flour, brown sugar, baking powder, salt and xanthan gum in a bowl with a spoon. Add the rice milk, oil and vanilla and mix well. Stir in the banana.

Pour about 1/4 cup of the batter onto a hot lightly greased griddle. Cook until bubbles appear on the surface and the underside is golden brown. Turn the pancake and cook until brown on the remaining side. Repeat the process with the remaining batter.

Prepare the pancakes and freeze in sealable plastic bags for future use, if desired. Reheat in a toaster oven for a quick and tasty breakfast.

Yield: 10 (1-pancake) servings

Allergy-Free
Nutritional Profiles 230–233

Gingersnap Pumpkin Cheesecake

Gingersnap Crust

3/4 cup gingersnap cookie crumbs

3/4 cup fat-free graham cracker crumbs

2 tablespoons granulated Splenda

1/4 cup (1/2 stick) unsalted butter, melted

Pumpkin Filling

24 ounces fat-free cream cheese, softened

1/2 cup granulated Splenda

1 1/2 cups canned solid-pack pumpkin

1/2 cup nonfat evaporated milk

1/3 cup maple syrup

1 tablespoon vanilla extract

1 tablespoon molasses

3/4 teaspoon cinnamon

1/2 teaspoon ground allspice

4 eggs

For the crust, combine the cookie crumbs, graham cracker crumbs, Splenda and butter in a bowl and stir with a fork until crumbly. Press over the bottom and 2 inches up the side of a greased and floured 8-inch springform pan.

For the filling, beat the cream cheese and Splenda in a mixing bowl until light and fluffy. Stir in the pumpkin. Add the evaporated milk, syrup, vanilla, molasses, cinnamon and allspice and beat until blended. Add the eggs one at a time, beating until smooth after each addition. Spread the filling over the prepared layer.

Bake in a preheated 325-degree oven for 1 1/2 hours or until the center of the cheesecake is set. Cool in the pan on a wire rack for 30 minutes. Chill, covered, for 8 to 10 hours.

Yield: 8 servings

Diabetic
Nutritional Profiles 230–233

Sugar-Free Cream Puffs

*This recipe is easy and fun to prepare. Smaller children can assist parents with
the preparation of these cream puffs and older teens can make them by themselves. They are
sugar-free and make a great dessert for diabetic children, adults, and grandparents.
They taste just like cream puffs from the bakery!*

1 cup water

1/2 cup (1 stick) butter

1 cup all-purpose flour

1 egg

1 small package vanilla sugar-free
pudding mix

Sugar-Free
Nutritional Profiles 230–233

Combine the water and butter in a saucepan. Cook until the butter melts. Bring just to a boil. Remove from the heat and whisk in the flour until blended. Pour into a mixing bowl and add the egg. Beat until blended.

Spoon the batter evenly into twenty-four greased muffin cups. Bake in a preheated 350-degree oven for 20 to 25 minutes or until the tops are golden brown. Let stand until cool. Use a spoon to poke holes in the tops of the puffs.

Prepare the pudding using the package directions. Pour the pudding into a sealable plastic bag and cut off one corner, creating a pastry bag.

Squeeze the pudding evenly into the puffs. Garnish with fresh blueberries. Serve immediately or chill, covered, in the refrigerator.

Yield: 24 cream puffs

Photograph for this recipe on page 210.

Egg-Free Cake

Send this cake to school with children who have egg allergies for birthday celebrations.

1 (2-layer) package any flavor cake mix

1 cup vanilla yogurt

3/4 cup water

Combine the cake mix, yogurt and water in a mixing bowl and beat until blended. Bake as directed on the package, adding 5 to 7 minutes to the bake time. Cool in the pan or pans on a wire rack. Freeze for future use, if desired. Thaw at room temperature.

Yield: 24 servings

Egg-Free
Nutritional Profiles 230–233

Low-Carb Pudding

1/2 cup whipping cream

1/2 cup (or more) water

8 ounces Philadelphia cream cheese, softened

1 large package sugar-free chocolate instant pudding mix or flavor of choice

Combine the cream, water and cream cheese in a blender or food processor. Process until smooth, adding water as needed for the desired consistency. Add the pudding mix gradually, processing constantly until blended. Chill until serving time.

Yield: 8 (1/2-cup) servings

Low-Carb
Nutritional Profiles 230–233

Dairy-Free Hot Chocolate

A delicious dairy-free drink you can enjoy on a cold winter day.

2 tablespoons sugar

1 tablespoon baking cocoa

1 cup plain or vanilla soy milk

Mix the sugar and baking cocoa in a large microwave-safe mug. Add the soy milk and whisk until blended.

Microwave for 1 to 2 minutes or until the desired temperature. Stir before serving. Vanilla soy milk adds a special flavor.

Yield: 1 serving

Dairy-Free
Nutritional Profiles 230–233

Spiced Iced Tea

6 cups water

1 teaspoon whole cloves

1 (1-inch) cinnamon stick

3 tea bags

3/4 cup orange juice

1/2 cup sugar

1 tablespoon lemon juice

Combine the water, cloves and cinnamon stick in a saucepan and bring to a boil. Remove from the heat and add the tea bags. Steep, covered, for 10 minutes. Strain, discarding the solids.

Combine the orange juice, sugar and lemon juice in a saucepan and bring to a boil. Cool slightly and pour into a large heatproof pitcher. Mix in the spiced tea. Chill, covered, in the refrigerator. Pour over ice in glasses.

Yield: 6 (1-cup) servings

Kosher
Nutritional Profiles 230–233

Sponsors

The Junior League of New Orleans, Inc., thanks the following sponsors for their generous donations, which helped underwrite *Crescent City Moons, Dishes and Spoons.*

Helping Hands
Lemle & Kelleher, L.L.P.

Whole Foods Market

Little Chefs
Brandon, Cris, Chaz, Noah, Beau, and Sebastian Bregman

Leah, Miller, Wilson, Elizabeth, and McCall Engelhardt

Anne, Terry, and Samantha Knister

The Gordon Kolb Family

Nell and Sorrell Lanier

Jace and Nyla Larsen

Erin and Hans Luetkemeier and Family

Kathleen, Kearny, Molly, and Lizzie Robert

Hallie and Rocky White

'94 Playgroup:

Gran, Luke, Conner, Matthew, Andrew, Turner, Allen, Peter, Morgan, and Robert

2008–2009 Junior League Interior Decorating Club

Bibs and Bottles
KitchenOlogy

nola baby magazine

The Savvy Gourmet

Chef Contributors

Thank you to our New Orleans "chefs" who graciously shared their "secret" recipes with us in honor of *the growing chef*.

John Besh of August, Besh Steak, Lüke, La Provence

Ryan Bowen of the New Orleans Hornets

Frank Brigtsen of Brigtsen's Restaurant

Gregg Collier of Red Fish Grill

Tommy D'Giovanni of Arnaud's

Joel Dondis of Sucré

Chip Flanagan of Ralph's on the Park

Tariq Hanna of Sucré

Molly Kimball of Ochsner's Elmwood Fitness Center

Jack Martinez of Dickie Brennan's Steakhouse

Chris Montero of BACCO

Darin Nesbit of Bourbon House

April Neujean of The Samuel J. Green Charter School Edible Schoolyard

Sean Payton of the New Orleans Saints

Vincent Pigna of Gelato Pazzo Caffè

Susan Spicer of Bayona

Jarod Tees of Lüke

Ben Thibodeaux of Palace Café

Poppy Tooker

Contributors List

Thank you to the following members and their friends and families for sharing their favorite recipes that fill the pages of *Crescent City Moons, Dishes and Spoons*.

Meg Baldwin	Holly Dalferes	Elizabeth Hailey
Jeanea Bandi	Colin James Dalton	Olivia Haverkamp
Charlotte Benton	Jordan Catherine Dalton	Chloe Helm
Diana Bercaw	Blanche Daniels	Andrew Henderson
Cris Bregman	Jennifer DiGiovanni	Ann Herren
Jeanne Harang Boughton	Natalie Donnelly	Meghan Hoffmann
Reed Bowman	Ann Dufrene	Nora V. Holmes
Karon Brown	Kerri Navo Duggan	Wesley Janssen
Amy Browne	Leah Engelhardt	Heather Johnson
Julie Buhrer	Enid Fahrenholt	Molly Kimball
Beverly Byrd	Meg Farris	Mary Jo Knappich
Claire Carr	Helen Fish	Catherine Koppel
Carla Catalano	Barb Fitzhugh	Karen Kuebel
Monica Chandler	Margaret Foster	Nell Lanier
Lori Christensen	Daphne Glindmeyer	Beth LeBlanc
Phoebe Cook	Jenny Gomez	Benjamin Link
Aidan Couvillon	Gwathmey Gomila	Amanda Lo
Blake Couvillon	Olivia Guider	Erin Luetkemeier
Bryce Couvillon	Amy Gutierrez	Cheron Mann

Octavio Mantilla

Brenda Marshall

Nancy Matulich

Allison McCammon

Christy McCann

Gina McMahon

Claudette Mendez

Rebecca Metzinger

Dominique Meyer

J. Matthew Miller III

Ryan Miller

Rose Milligan

Ron Mills

Patsy Mitchell

Amy Moore

Cherie Moore

Eva Morris

Leigh Moss

Linda Mouchacca

Caroline Noya

Sherri Zeller O'Bell

Koki Ogawa

Judy Paine

Brooke Parry

Leslie Perchall

Annie Phillips

Allison Plaisance

Ashley Pugeau

Maylee Reese

Max Reese

Tara Reese

Courtney Rivé

Kathleen Vogt Robert

Allison Russell

Pablo Sanchez

Rita Medellin Sanchez

Erin Saucier

Linda Schroeder

Robyn Schwarz

Amy Schwarzenbach

Alison Scott

Eva Seligman

Penny Synnott

Debbie Tabb

Dixie Taylor

Susan Taylor

Caitlin Tobin

Mary Catherine Toso

Claire Trask

Jodie Trask

Jennifer Umbright

Archer VanDenburgh

Beau VanDenburgh

Jennifer Van Vrancken

Courtney Walker

Cheryl Webster

Caroline Wendt

Mary Wendt

Hallie White

Sarah Wittenbrink

Charlee Williamson

Jeannie Williamson

Tracy Woodie

Jennifer Zeringue

Shannon Zink

Junior Taste Testers

Thank you to the following *growing chefs,* who provided their discerning palates
for ensuring our selection of the most-favored recipes.

Patrick Bandi	Koki Ogawa
Beau Bregman	Dottie Phillips
Chaz Bregman	Niel Phillips
Noah Bregman	Marguerite Schwarz
Casey Carr	Evan Schwarzenbach
Claire Carr	Georgia Kate Scott
Price A. Combes	Grayson Scott
Jack Cook	Jack Trask
William Cook	Jake Trask
Beata Desselle	Joseph Trask
Brian Fish, Jr.	Garrett G. Walker
Travis Fish	Marshall K. Walker
Alexis Hernandez	David Webster
Cali Jane Luetkemeier	Dex Webster
Mary Kate Luetkemeier	Don Webster
Cate McCammon	Nicholas White

2008–2009 Dino Class at Edisen House

Recipe Basics

1

Ingredients in cans or jars are undrained unless specified
differently in the recipe.

2

Vegetables and fruits are of medium size unless specified differently.

3

Vegetables and fruits with inedible peels
(for example, bananas, winter squash, avocados) are to be peeled.

4

Vegetables and fruits are fresh unless specified differently.

5

Sugar is granulated unless specified differently.

6

Horseradish and mustard are prepared unless specified differently.

7

Nuts, seeds, and dried legumes with inedible shells are to be shelled.

Nutritional Profiles

Crescent City
Coos

Crescent City
Cuties

Crescent City
Cool Kids

Crescent City
Conditional Cooking

Pg #	Recipe Title (Approx Per Serving)	Cal	T Fat (g)	Sat Fat (g)	Chol (mg)	Sod (mg)	Carbo (g)	Fiber (g)	Sugars (g)	Prot (g)
20	Tofu Cheerios Snack	111	4.9	0.9	0	91	9.9	2	1	9.3
21	Baby Beau's Butternut Squash Soup	42	0.5	0	2	135	8.9	1.6	4.7	1.2
22	Banana Avocado Baby Food	198	9	2	5	63	27	5	15	6
22	Fruit Salad	69	2.9	0	0	2	11.4	2.6	5.6	0.9
23	Tropical Fruit Treat	76	3.8	0.5	0	4	11.4	3.4	4.8	1
24	Beef Stroganoff	127	9.5	1.8	22	300	3.3	0	0.5	7.2
25	Chicken Noodle Delight	62	1.1	0	21	121	6.1	0.6	0.7	6.5
26	Chicken and Squash Dinner	68	0.9	0	22	20	6.6	1.1	1.2	8.8
26	Turkey Orzo	253	8.1	2.8	46	183	26.3	1.5	3	18.2
27	Salmon Spinach and Peas	108	5.6	1.1	27	316	3.3	1	1.4	10.8
27	Quesadillas	110	5.7	3.6	15	150	7.5	1.3	4.2	7.5
30	Ga-Ga Guacamole	61	5.5	0.8	0	12	3.3	2.5	0	0.8
30	Pumpkin Spinach Pasta	135	4.4	0.7	21	107	20.6	1.8	2.1	4
31	Cauliflower Lasagna	90	0.7	0	21	123	17.4	0.7	1.2	3.7
31	Popeye Pasta	193	7.5	4.3	47	175	22.9	0	1.1	8.4
32	Rosemary Potatoes	119	7.4	1.1	0	291	12.2	1.3	1	1.7
32	Squash and Fruit Purée	105	0.2	0	0	4	27.5	3.6	16.1	1.4
33	Ratatouille	56	3.9	0.5	0	107	4.7	1.5	2.7	1.9
34	Green Vegetable Medley	62	4.9	0.7	0	143	3.8	1.5	1.4	1.4

Pg #	Recipe Title (Approx Per Serving)	Cal	T Fat (g)	Sat Fat (g)	Chol (mg)	Sod (mg)	Carbo (g)	Fiber (g)	Sugars (g)	Prot (g)
35	Yellow Vegetable Medley	64	2.6	0	0	144	9.6	2	3.5	1.1
38	Orange Julius	92	1	0.5	3	18	18.9	0	17.4	1.9
38	Strawberry Princess Punch	170	0.1	0	0	17	43.8	0	42	0.2
39	Gourmet Granola	244	11.5	2.3	0	42	34.8	2.8	22.2	3.9
40	Quick Kabobs	90	4.6	3.3	9	53	10.9	1.6	6.6	2.7
40	Sam's Strawberry Sandwiches	181	7.3	4.3	21	302	23.3	0.9	2.4	5.9
41	Tutti-Frutti Tacos	181	8.7	1.8	0	84	22.3	5	7.2	5.4
42	Dill Pickle Soup	166	13.9	6.3	33	794	2.1	0	0	8
43	Pepper Boat Salads	101	6.7	4.1	21	98	5.5	1.6	3.3	4.8
44	Beefy Noodles	449	16.3	5.9	106	4290	51.2	3.5	4.3	25.9
45	Marguerite's Meatballs	217	6.8	2.4	129	572	11	2.4	4	27.9
46	Kids' Favorite Meat Loaf	288	11.3	4.4	140	740	6.3	0	3	37.8
47	Homemade Sloppy Joes	387	7.8	2.5	67	770	49	1.8	22.2	29.7
48	Oven-Baked Barbecue Ribs	507	30.2	10.7	175	416	10.3	0	7.4	45.1
48	Noodles and Ham	290	10.7	5.5	82	335	36.3	1.8	1.3	11.9
49	Ham Biscuits	163	9.1	4.7	26	346	14.4	0.8	1.7	6.1
50	Muffuletta Pasta	427	24.9	13.1	100	1211	25.4	1	0	25.5
51	Italian-Style Chicken Nuggets	258	12.1	6.4	95	322	6.8	0	0.7	29
51	Coconut Chicken Nuggets	266	12.9	7.3	93	338	8.1	0.9	0.9	28
52	Honey Mustard Dipping Sauce	130	0	0	0	2	35	0	34.8	0.1
52	Chicken Poppy Seed	380	12	10.7	101	514	18.8	0	2.1	27
53	Children's Fried Rice	384	6.7	1.8	143	282	36.5	1.6	0	41.3
56	Kid-Friendly Easy Chili	364	11.9	2.7	58	313	36.3	8.4	2.1	28.3
57	Yummy Tuna Casserole	267	7.2	3.1	60	189	32.7	0	1.2	17.1
57	Inside-Out Sandwiches	273	9.8	4.1	37	786	31.7	1.7	2.9	13.6
58	Tootie's Elvis Sandwich	435	18.2	3.8	0	413	58.2	7.1	29.5	15.9
58	Glazed Carrots	116	6	3.7	15	191	16.1	2.1	11.4	0.8
59	Natsha's Apple Cheese Casserole	511	28	10.5	40	437	55.7	1.8	36	11.3
60	Oven-Baked Cauliflower	198	10.7	1.7	8	478	23	3.3	5.6	4.5
60	Zucchini Crispies	120	6.9	1.1	5	297	13.3	1	2.9	2.3
61	Biscuits	180	11.1	3.4	1	270	17.7	0.6	1	2.8
62	Corn Bread	218	5.6	2.9	40	376	39.2	2	13.8	4.8
63	Georgia's Sweet Potato Apple Muffins	96	0.6	0	16	162	21	1.1	10.8	2
64	Whole Grain Waffles	330	15.3	5.8	72	83	43.5	1.5	20.8	6.1

Pg #	Recipe Title (Approx Per Serving)	Cal	T Fat (g)	Sat Fat (g)	Chol (mg)	Sod (mg)	Carbo (g)	Fiber (g)	Sugars (g)	Prot (g)
65	Pumpkin Dip	136	4.1	2.5	12	99	24.2	1.9	10.6	1.3
65	Chocolate Popcorn Clusters	247	15.2	5.4	8	29	24.2	2.6	11.4	6.3
66	S'mores Pops	230	7.6	4.9	5	87	37.8	1	24.9	2.5
66	Zebras	214	0.7	0	0	814	51.3	1	45.6	0.7
67	Frozen Banana Pops	316	14.1	6.9	7	29	42.5	4.6	26.4	6.2
67	Madeline's Fresh Lemon Ice Cream	76	0	0	0	0	20.1	0	19.1	0.1
68	Blueberry Oatmeal Bars	234	12.4	2	0	184	27.7	1.8	8.5	3.3
69	Yogurt Pie	264	13.3	7.8	3	162	33.7	0.7	27.5	3.9
72	Berry Banana Smoothie	258	2.8	1	4	49	55.7	3.8	44	7.4
72	Garden Dip	45	2.1	0.9	7	133	2.9	0	0.8	3.6
73	Fruit Salsa and Cinnamon Chips	217	1.2	0	0	11	53.9	9.1	34.6	2.6
74	Jen's Vegetable Square Appetizers	344	17.7	9.5	46	602	34.7	2.1	5	12.3
75	Creamy Tortilla Soup	286	15.6	8	64	596	16	1.3	2.7	20.5
76	Peach Salsa Chicken Salad	376	12.9	5	61	87	44.6	4.4	20.4	21.1
77	Tricolor Pasta Salad	216	9.3	2	9	644	26.7	6.2	4.7	7.6
78	Cowboy Salad	258	2.8	1.4	6	184	38.7	9.7	3	19.7
79	Catalina Salad Dressing	180	13.6	1.9	0	347	15.2	0	14.8	0.2
80	Roasted Pecan Balsamic Dressing	114	11.4	1.9	3	60	2.7	0	2.2	0.8
81	Crispy Noodle Coleslaw	352	29.3	3.1	0	308	20.5	2.5	7.9	5.6
82	Noah's Tender Slow-Cooker Brisket	219	6.3	3	33	723	31.6	0.8	27.5	11
83	Italian Beef	422	14.1	5.5	202	150	0	0	0	68.9
84	Awesome Spaghetti	418	13.8	7	130	734	25.7	1.3	6.8	46.2
85	Pork Chops and Apples	508	30.6	14.4	96	2466	38.8	1.5	21.5	19.4
86	Spaghetti alla Carbonara	689	33.7	9.6	356	1111	64.1	0	0.9	31.4
87	Chaz's Chicken and Dumplings	417	17.1	9.3	122	546	25.5	1.1	0.9	37.9
88	Chicken and Broccoli Risotto	421	10.9	5.9	106	1061	44.3	2	1.9	36
89	Chicken Piccata	359	13.4	5.3	112	382	15.8	0.8	1	37.2
90	Creamy Chicken Lasagna	307	10.9	5.9	77	420	24.6	0	3.9	26.4
91	Feta-Stuffed Chicken	303	14	4.4	110	308	4.2	2.1	1	39.6
94	Homemade Chicken Potpie	489	26.7	4.3	33	752	45	4.6	6	17.7
95	Pita Pocket Sandwich	312	8.1	4.1	58	432	32.9	1.6	1.3	25.6
95	Baked Catfish	328	4.1	0.9	116	1594	21.1	1.5	2.3	48.6
96	Crawfish Pasta	581	31.6	18.5	248	538	47.7	0.7	1.2	26.6
97	Crawfish Pie	345	27.7	13.2	110	389	15.1	0.6	1.6	8.6

Pg #	Recipe Title (Approx Per Serving)	Cal	T Fat (g)	Sat Fat (g)	Chol (mg)	Sod (mg)	Carbo (g)	Fiber (g)	Sugars (g)	Prot (g)
98	Shrimp Appaloosa	406	16.9	3	147	667	40	1.2	1.4	21.7
99	Jambalaya	632	30	8.6	270	1090	29.8	1.4	2.6	56.9
100	Cheesy Eggplant "Lasagna"	205	7.1	3.5	16	461	28.2	12	13.8	10.7
101	Daniel's Penne	405	24	7.7	73	214	35.8	0	0.8	12.2
102	Spaghetti Casserole	358	14.4	7.6	143	499	36.8	0.9	2.8	20
103	Mom's Marinara Sauce	86	6.4	0.9	2	17	7.3	1.9	4.2	1.2
104	Healthy Spaghetti Sauce	165	3.8	1.4	50	174	13.4	2.7	6.4	19.8
105	Creole Scrambled Eggs	397	20.7	6.1	247	168	38	0.8	0.7	13.8
106	Baked Peach French Toast	174	9.1	3.3	14	130	21.1	1.7	13	3.4
107	Puffy Potatoes	65	2.4	0.7	17	57	8.7	1.3	0.7	2.2
108	Squash Potato Casserole	261	12.7	6.4	71	376	28.3	3.9	3.1	9.6
109	Roasted Squash and Potato Pie	206	7.2	2.7	11	354	28.2	3.3	2.4	8.5
110	Spinach Casserole	190	11.3	6.2	87	563	16	1.6	2.3	7.3
111	Tomato Zucchini Tian	197	15.7	3	6	108	11.7	4.1	5.9	4.8
204	Healthy Snack Granola Bars	196	6	2.5	0	29	32.3	3.9	12.4	4.6
205	Basil Zucchini Soup	45	2.8	0	0	134	3.8	1	1.7	2
206	Olivia's Feel-Good Chicken Soup	229	3	0.8	51	375	25.8	2.2	2.9	23.3
207	Chicken Stock	10	0.6	0	0	764	0.7	0	0.7	0.7
208	Orange Jell-O Salad	132	10.8	6.5	0	7	9.1	0.7	8.1	0.9
209	Grilled Asian Steak Salad	160	7	2	20	250	11	3	0	15
212	Tuna and Veggie Salad	33.1	20.6	3.3	26	120	10.7	2.5	7.5	23.5
213	Beef Tzimmes	371	10.2	3.9	144	123	17.8	1.5	14.6	50
214	Wheatballs and Spaghetti Squash	340	16.4	3.9	126	335	10.1	4.7	0	36
215	Baked Flounder in Dill Sauce	84.4	2.3	0.4	0	353.1	2	0.1	0.9	12.2
216	Sesame Tilapia	219	15.2	2.5	56	622	0	0	0	21.3
217	Cauliflower Soufflé	152	11.2	5	30	213	11.1	0.9	1.6	2.8
218	Hearty Grits	181	11.2	7.4	32	581	7.9	1.3	3.5	12.5
219	Pancakes	103	3.2	0	0	12	17.6	1.2	1.2	1.1
220	Gingersnap Pumpkin Cheesecake	310	11	5	130	550	34	3	18	19
221	Sugar-Free Cream Puffs	118	4.2	2.5	18	815	18.7	0	0	1
222	Egg-Free Cake	99	2.5	0	1	152	17.7	0	12.6	1.5
222	Low-Carb Pudding	143	14.5	9.1	48	89	1.2	0	0	2.5
223	Dairy-Free Hot Chocolate	241	7	2	0	138	46	5	37	7
223	Spiced Iced Tea	80	0.1	0	0	8	20.1	0	19.3	0.2

Index

Allergy-Free
Pancakes, 219

Almonds
Crispy Noodle Coleslaw, 81
English Trifle, 172
Gourmet Granola, 39

Appetizers. See also Dips; Snacks
Cheese Yummies, 121
Jen's Vegetable Square
Appetizers, 74
N'awlins Deviled Eggs, 115
Savory Cheese and Pimento
Appetizer, 120
Virginia's Jalapeño Cheese Ball, 119

Apple
Fruit Salsa and Cinnamon Chips, 73
Georgia's Sweet Potato Apple
Muffins, 63
Natsha's Apple Cheese
Casserole, 59
Pork Chops and Apples, 85

Avocado
Guacamole, 149
Peach Salsa Chicken Salad, 76

Baby Food
Baby Beau's Butternut Squash
Soup, 21
Banana Avocado Baby Food, 22
Beef Stroganoff, 24
Cauliflower Lasagna, 31
Chicken and Squash Dinner, 26
Chicken Noodle Delight, 25
Fruit Salad, 22
Ga-Ga Guacamole, 30
Green Vegetable Medley, 34
Popeye Pasta, 31
Pumpkin Spinach Pasta, 30
Quesadillas, 27
Ratatouille, 33
Rosemary Potatoes, 32

Salmon Spinach and Peas, 27
Squash and Fruit Purée, 32
Tofu Cheerios Snack, 20
Tropical Fruit Treat, 23
Turkey Orzo, 26
Yellow Vegetable Medley, 35

Bacon/Pancetta
Bigos, 158
Coq au Vin, 160
Dill Pickle Soup, 42
Hot Cheesy Bacon Dip, 117
Oyster Chowder, 182
Spaghetti alla Carbonara, 86
Wheatballs and Spaghetti
Squash, 214

Banana
Banana Caramel Pie, 142
Bercaw Boys' Banana
Bread, 128
Berry Banana Smoothie, 72
Chocolate Chip-Banana
Cake, 129
Frozen Banana Pops, 67
Million Dollar Pie, 145
Purple Passion Frozen
Drink, 114
Tootie's Elvis Sandwich, 58

Beans
Black Bean Dip, 116
Cowboy Salad, 78
Kid-Friendly Easy Chili, 56
Maque Choux, 188
Mexican Five-Layer Dip, 117

Beef. See also Ground Beef
Beef Tzimmes, 213
Grilled Asian Steak Salad, 209
Honey's Hungarian Goulash, 153
Italian Beef, 83
Noah's Tender Slow-Cooker
Brisket, 82
Sauerbraten, 154

Beverages
Berry Banana Smoothie, 72
Dairy-Free Hot Chocolate, 223
Orange Julius, 38
Purple Passion Frozen
Drink, 114
Spiced Iced Tea, 223

Beverages, Punch
Party Punch, 114
Strawberry Princess Punch, 38
Witches' Brew, 115

Blueberry
Blueberry Oatmeal Bars, 68
Blueberry Pancakes, 196
Fruit Salsa and Cinnamon Chips, 73
Sparkling Watermelon Soup, 178

Breads
Baked Peach French Toast, 106
Bercaw Boys' Banana Bread, 128
Biscuits, 61
Blueberry Pancakes, 196
Calas, 197
Corn Bread, 62
Georgia's Sweet Potato Apple
Muffins, 63
Grandma Gert's Orange
Biscuits, 127
Pancakes, 219
Shortcake, 196
Soda Bread, 171
Whole Grain Waffles, 64

Broccoli
Chicken and Broccoli
Risotto, 88
Jen's Vegetable Square
Appetizers, 74
Tricolor Pasta Salad, 77

Brunch. See also Breads;
Egg Dishes
Christmas Morning Pie, 125

Cabbage
Bigos, 158
Mardi Gras Salad, 122

Cakes
Chocolate Chip-Banana Cake, 129
Citrus Yogurt Cake, 132
Egg-Free Cake, 222
Great-Grandmother's Red Velvet
Cake, 136
King Cake for Kids, 133
Pineapple Goo Cake, 135
Sally's Mandarin Orange-Pineapple
Cake, 134

Candy
Easy Chocolate Truffles, 198
Microwave Pralines, 137

Carrots
Beef Tzimmes, 213
Chicken Stock, 207
Coq au Vin, 160
Glazed Carrots, 58
Grilled Asian Steak Salad, 209
Homemade Chicken Potpie, 94
Mom's Marinara Sauce, 103
Olivia's Feel-Good Chicken
Soup, 206
Tricolor Pasta Salad, 77

Cauliflower
Cauliflower Soufflé, 217
Jen's Vegetable Square
Appetizers, 74
Oven-Baked Cauliflower, 60
Tricolor Pasta Salad, 77

Chicken
Adobo, 165
Arroz con Pollo, 159
Cajun-Style Chicken Breast with
Chili Bean Maque Choux, 186
Chaz's Chicken and Dumplings, 87
Chicken and Broccoli Risotto, 88

Chicken Nuggets, 51
Chicken Piccata, 89
Chicken Poppy Seed, 52
Chicken Stock, 207
Children's Fried Rice, 53
Coconut Chicken Nuggets, 51
Coq au Vin, 160
Couscous Salad, 152
Creamy Chicken Lasagna, 90
Creamy Tortilla Soup, 75
Feta-Stuffed Chicken, 91
Grandpa Pablo's Fideos con
Pollo, 161
Homemade Chicken Potpie, 94
Italian-Style Chicken Nuggets, 51
Jambalaya, 99
Jerk Chicken, 164
Olivia's Feel-Good Chicken
Soup, 206
Organic Chicken and Matzo Ball
Soup, 179
Peach Salsa Chicken Salad, 76

Chocolate
Chocolate Chip-Banana Cake, 129
Chocolate Popcorn Clusters, 65
Dairy-Free Hot Chocolate, 223
Easy Chocolate Truffles, 198
Frozen Banana Pops, 67
Lisa's Peanut Butter Squares, 137
Low-Carb Pudding, 222
Magical Mocha Wands, 141
Microwave Chocolate Pie, 143
Mr. Ralph's Ice Cream
Sandwiches, 200
S'mores Pops, 66
Zebras, 66

Coconut
Coconut Chicken Nuggets, 51
Coconut Macaroons, 139
Gourmet Granola, 39
Healthy Snack Granola Bars, 204
Million Dollar Pie, 145
Pineapple Goo Cake, 135

Cookies
Baby Fingers, 142
Coconut Macaroons, 139
Lace Oatmeal Cookies, 139
Magical Mocha Wands, 141
Melting Moments, 140
Perfect Cookie, The, 199
Rugelach, 174

Cookies, Bar
Blueberry Oatmeal Bars, 68
Healthy Snack Granola Bars, 204
Lisa's Peanut Butter
Squares, 137
Pan Dulce, 175
Pumpkin Squares, 138

Corn
Corn Bread, 62
Homemade Chicken Potpie, 94
Maque Choux, 188

Crawfish
Crawfish Pasta, 96
Crawfish Pie, 97

Dairy-Free
Dairy-Free Hot Chocolate, 223
Healthy Snack Granola Bars, 204

Desserts. *See also* Cakes; Candy;
Cookies; Cookies, Bar;
Frostings/Icings; Pies, Dessert
Baklava, 173
Chocolate Popcorn Clusters, 65
English Trifle, 172
Gingersnap Crust, 220
Gingersnap Pumpkin
Cheesecake, 220
Low-Carb Pudding, 222
Natsha's Apple Cheese
Casserole, 59
Palace Café Ponchatoula
Strawberry Shortcake, 194
Pumpkin Dip, 65

S'mores Pops, 66
Sugar-Free Cream Puffs, 221
Zebras, 66

Desserts, Frozen
Frozen Banana Pops, 67
Madeline's Fresh Lemon
Ice Cream, 67
Mr. Ralph's Ice Cream
Sandwiches, 200

Diabetic
Baked Flounder in
Dill Sauce, 215
Gingersnap Pumpkin
Cheesecake, 220
Grilled Asian Steak Salad, 209

Dips
Black Bean Dip, 116
Fruit Salsa and Cinnamon
Chips, 73
Garden Dip, 72
Guacamole, 149
Hot Cheesy Bacon Dip, 117
Lincoln Lee's Marshmallow
Fruit Dip, 118
Mamaw's Chive Dip, 116
Mexican Five-Layer Dip, 117
Pumpkin Dip, 65
Raspberry Billy Goat Dip, 118
Tzatziki, 148

Dressings/Vinaigrettes
Asian Dressing, 209
Catalina Salad Dressing, 79
Coleslaw Dressing, 81
Roasted Pecan Balsamic
Dressing, 80
Soy Vinaigrette, 122

Egg Dishes
Brunch Soufflé, 124
Creole Scrambled Eggs, 105
N'awlins Deviled Eggs, 115

Egg-Free
Egg-Free Cake, 222

Eggplant
Cheesy Eggplant "Lasagna," 100
Tomato Zucchini Tian, 111

Fish. See also Tuna
Baked Catfish, 95
Baked Flounder in Dill Sauce, 215
Blackened Redfish Burgers, 188
Sesame Tilapia, 216

Frostings/Icings
Butter Frosting, 140
Cream Cheese Icing, 138
Icing, 135
Pineapple Frosting, 134
Red Velvet Icing, 136

Fruit. See also Apple; Avocado;
Banana; Blueberry; Coconut;
Kiwifruit; Orange; Peach;
Pineapple; Pumpkin; Raspberry;
Strawberry
Beef Tzimmes, 213
Berry Banana Smoothie, 72
Citrus Yogurt Cake, 132
Healthy Snack Granola Bars, 204
Madeline's Fresh Lemon
Ice Cream, 67
Quick Kabobs, 40
Sparkling Watermelon Soup, 178
Tutti-Frutti Tacos, 41

Grains. See Grits; Rice

Grits
Cheese Grits, 123
Cheesy Grits, 192
Hearty Grits, 218

Ground Beef
Awesome Spaghetti, 84
Beefy Noodles, 44

Bobotie, 155
Cowboy Salad, 78
Grandma's Swedish
Meatballs, 156
Healthy Spaghetti Sauce, 104
Homemade Sloppy Joes, 47
Italian Wedding Soup, 150
Kids' Favorite Meat Loaf, 46
Lasagna, 184
Marguerite's Meatballs, 45
Marvelous Miniature
Meat Loaves, 185

Ham
Christmas Morning Pie, 125
Ham Biscuits, 49
Inside-Out Sandwiches, 57
Muffuletta Pasta, 50
Noodles and Ham, 48

Kiwifruit
Fruit Salsa and Cinnamon
Chips, 73
Million Dollar Pie, 145

Kosher
Beef Tzimmes, 213
Spiced Iced Tea, 223

Low-Carb
Low-Carb Pudding, 222
Sesame Tilapia, 216
Tuna and Veggie
Salad, 212

Low-Fat, Low-Carb, High Fiber
Wheatballs and Spaghetti
Squash, 214

Mushrooms
Bigos, 158
Cheesy Eggplant "Lasagna," 100
Coq au Vin, 160
Creamy Chicken Lasagna, 90
Shrimp Appaloosa, 98

Nuts. *See also* Almonds; Pecans
Baklava, 173
Gourmet Granola, 39

Orange
Grandma Gert's Orange
Biscuits, 127
Orange Jell-O Salad, 208
Orange Julius, 38
Sally's Mandarin Orange-Pineapple
Cake, 134

Pasta
Awesome Spaghetti, 84
Beefy Noodles, 44
Cauliflower Soufflé, 217
Couscous Salad, 152
Crawfish Pasta, 96
Creamy Chicken Lasagna, 90
Daniel's Penne, 101
Grandma's Swedish
Meatballs, 156
Grandpa Pablo's Fideos con
Pollo, 161
Healthy Spaghetti Sauce, 104
Italian Wedding Soup, 150
Lasagna, 184
Mom's Marinara Sauce, 103
Muffuletta Pasta, 50
Noodles and Ham, 48
Shrimp Felicia, 192
Spaghetti alla Carbonara, 86
Spaghetti Casserole, 102
Tricolor Pasta Salad, 77
Yummy Tuna Casserole, 57

Peach
Baked Peach French Toast, 106
Peach Salsa Chicken Salad, 76

Peanut Butter
Lisa's Peanut Butter
Squares, 137
Tootie's Elvis Sandwich, 58
Tutti-Frutti Tacos, 41

Peanuts
Chocolate Popcorn Clusters, 65
Mardi Gras Salad, 122

Peas
Asian Sugar Snap Peas, 166
Grilled Asian Steak Salad, 209
Homemade Chicken Potpie, 94
Noodles and Ham, 48
Tricolor Pasta Salad, 77

Pecans
Baked Sweet Potatoes with
Pecan Butter, 193
Banana Caramel Pie, 142
Healthy Snack Granola Bars, 204
Magical Mocha Wands, 141
Microwave Pralines, 137
Million Dollar Pie, 145
Pan Dulce, 175
Pecan Pie, 144
Pineapple Goo Cake, 135
Raspberry Billy Goat Dip, 118
Roasted Pecan Balsamic
Dressing, 80

Pies, Dessert
Banana Caramel Pie, 142
Meringue, 143
Microwave Chocolate Pie, 143
Million Dollar Pie, 145
Pecan Pie, 144
Pink Lemonade Pie, 144
Yogurt Pie, 69

Pies, Savory
Christmas Morning Pie, 125
Crawfish Pie, 97
Homemade Chicken Potpie, 94
Roasted Squash and Potato Pie, 109
Vidalia Onion Pie, 126

Pineapple
Baby Fingers, 142
Million Dollar Pie, 145

Orange Jell-O Salad, 208
Pineapple Frosting, 134
Pineapple Goo Cake, 135
Sally's Mandarin Orange-Pineapple
Cake, 134

Pork. *See also* Bacon/Pancetta;
Ham; Sausage
Bigos, 158
N'awlins Deviled Eggs, 115
Oven-Baked Barbecue Ribs, 48
Pork Chops and Apples, 85

Potatoes
Coq au Vin, 160
Crash Hot Potatoes, 167
Czechoslovakian Potato
Dumplings, 170
Dill Pickle Soup, 42
Homemade Chicken Potpie, 94
Honey's Hungarian Goulash, 153
LSU Potatoes, 123
Oyster Chowder, 182
Puffy Potatoes, 107
Roasted Squash and Potato Pie, 109
Squash Potato Casserole, 108

Poultry. *See* Chicken; Turkey

Pumpkin
Gingersnap Pumpkin
Cheesecake, 220
Pumpkin Dip, 65
Pumpkin Squares, 138

Raspberry
English Trifle, 172
Fruit Salsa and Cinnamon Chips, 73
Raspberry Billy Goat Dip, 118

Rice
Adobo, 165
Arroz con Pollo, 159
Calas, 197
Chicken and Broccoli Risotto, 88

Children's Fried Rice, 53
Creole Scrambled Eggs, 105
Jambalaya, 99
Olivia's Feel-Good Chicken
   Soup, 206
Saag Paneer, 168
Shrimp Appaloosa, 98

Salads
   Couscous Salad, 152
   Orange Jell-O Salad, 208
   Pepper Boat Salads, 43
   Sesame Sweet-and-Tangy
      Cucumbers, 151
   Tricolor Pasta Salad, 77

Salads, Main Dish
   Cowboy Salad, 78
   Grilled Asian Steak Salad, 209
   Peach Salsa Chicken Salad, 76
   Tuna and Veggie Salad, 212

Salads, Vegetable
   Crispy Noodle Coleslaw, 81
   Mardi Gras Salad, 122

Sandwiches
   Blackened Redfish Burgers, 188
   Ham Biscuits, 49
   Homemade Sloppy Joes, 47
   Inside-Out Sandwiches, 57
   Pita Pocket Sandwich, 95
   Sam's Strawberry Sandwiches, 40
   Tootie's Elvis Sandwich, 58

Sauces
   Healthy Spaghetti Sauce, 104
   Honey Mustard Dipping Sauce, 52
   Mom's Marinara Sauce, 103
   Tzatziki, 148

Sausage
   Bigos, 158
   Inside-Out Sandwiches, 57
   Jambalaya, 99

Muffuletta Pasta, 50
Slow-Cooked Louisiana Shrimp
   and Andouille over Grits, 190

Seafood. See Fish; Shellfish

Shellfish. See also Crawfish; Shrimp
   Oyster Chowder, 182

Shrimp
   Jambalaya, 99
   Shrimp Appaloosa, 98
   Shrimp Felicia, 192
   Shrimp Stock, 192
   Slow-Cooked Louisiana Shrimp
      and Andouille over Grits, 190

Snacks. See also Sandwiches
   Chocolate Chip-Banana Cake, 129
   Chocolate Popcorn Clusters, 65
   Gourmet Granola, 39
   Quick Kabobs, 40
   Tutti-Frutti Tacos, 41

Soups
   Basil Zucchini Soup, 205
   Bourbon House Butternut Squash
      Bisque, 181
   Chicken Stock, 207
   Creamy Tortilla Soup, 75
   Dill Pickle Soup, 42
   Italian Wedding Soup, 150
   Olivia's Feel-Good Chicken
      Soup, 206
   Organic Chicken and Matzo Ball
      Soup, 179
   Oyster Chowder, 182
   Shrimp Stock, 192
   Sparkling Watermelon Soup, 178
   Turtle Soup, 180

Spinach
   Beefy Noodles, 44
   Blueberry Oatmeal Bars, 68
   Hearty Grits, 218

Marguerite's Meatballs, 45
Saag Paneer, 168
Spinach Casserole, 110
Turtle Soup, 180

Squash
   Bourbon House Butternut Squash
      Bisque, 181
   Roasted Squash and Potato Pie, 109
   Squash Potato Casserole, 108
   Wheatballs and Spaghetti
      Squash, 214

Strawberry
   Fruit Salsa and Cinnamon
      Chips, 73
   Palace Café Ponchatoula
      Strawberry Shortcake, 194
   Purple Passion Frozen Drink, 114
   Sam's Strawberry Sandwiches, 40
   Strawberry Princess Punch, 38

Sugar-Free
   Sugar-Free Cream Puffs, 221

Sweet Potatoes
   Baked Sweet Potatoes with
      Pecan Butter, 193
   Beef Tzimmes, 213
   Georgia's Sweet Potato Apple
      Muffins, 63

Tomatoes
   Bigos, 158
   Cheesy Eggplant "Lasagna," 100
   Couscous Salad, 152
   Cowboy Salad, 78
   Daniel's Penne, 101
   Grandpa Pablo's Fideos con
      Pollo, 161
   Grilled Asian Steak Salad, 209
   Jambalaya, 99
   Jen's Vegetable Square
      Appetizers, 74
   Kid-Friendly Easy Chili, 56

Lasagna, 184
Mom's Marinara Sauce, 103
Organic Chicken and Matzo Ball
   Soup, 179
Pepper Boat Salads, 43
Saag Paneer, 168
Slow-Cooked Louisiana Shrimp
   and Andouille over Grits, 190
Tomato Zucchini Tian, 111
Turtle Soup, 180
Yummy Tuna Casserole, 57

Tuna
Tuna and Veggie Salad, 212
Yummy Tuna Casserole, 57

Turkey
Inside-Out Sandwiches, 57
Kid-Friendly Easy Chili, 56
Pita Pocket Sandwich, 95
Wheatballs and Spaghetti
   Squash, 214

Vegetables. *See also* Beans; Broccoli;
   Cabbage; Carrots; Cauliflower;
   Corn; Eggplant; Mushrooms;
   Peas; Pies, Savory; Potatoes;
   Salads, Vegetable; Spinach;
   Squash; Sweet Potatoes;
   Tomatoes; Zucchini
Vidalia Onion Pie, 126

Vegetarian
Basil Zucchini Soup, 205
Cauliflower Soufflé, 217

When You're Sick
Chicken Stock, 207
Hearty Grits, 218
Olivia's Feel-Good Chicken
   Soup, 206
Orange Jell-O Salad, 208

Zucchini
Basil Zucchini Soup, 205
Tomato Zucchini Tian, 111
Zucchini Crispies, 60

For additional copies of

Crescent City Moons, Dishes and Spoons

or for order information on any of
The Junior League of New Orleans, Inc., cookbooks,
please contact

The Junior League of New Orleans, Inc.
504.891.5845
www.jlno.org